Liliuokalani

Lili'uokalani

A ROYAL ALBUM

2/5/2020

To Joshua

In Honor of Hawaii's Last Queen!

ALLAN SEIDEN

Mutual Publishing

All photographs are from the collections of the
Hawaiian Legacy Archives unless otherwise noted.

ISBN-13: 978-1939487-81-0
Library of Congress Catalog Card Number: 2017909654
Design by Jane Gillespie and Allan Seiden
First Printing, October 2017
Second Printing, June 2018

Mutual Publishing, LLC
1215 Center Street, Suite 210
Honolulu, Hawai‘i 96816
Ph: (808) 732-1709
Fax: (808) 734-4094
e-mail: info@mutualpublishing.com
www.mutualpublishing.com

Printed in South Korea

Contents

Lili'uokalani's

ROYAL FAMILY TREE

More than her siblings, Lili'uokalani could claim family links to both the Kalākaua and Kamehameha dynasties. As hānai to Kamehameha's granddaughter, Konia, and her links to Kamehameha's daughter, Kīna'u, Lili'uokalani was a genealogical member of the Kamehameha family by the traditions of old Hawai'i. The below text appears without Hawaiian diacritics as written by Lili'uokalani. The royal lineage appears in **bold**.

ON HER FATHER'S (KAPAAKEA) SIDE

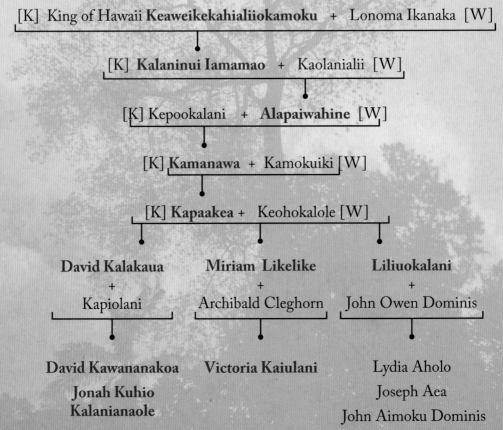

[K] King of Hawaii **Keaweikekahialiiokamoku** + Lonoma Ikanaka [W]

[K] **Kalaninui Iamamao** + Kaolanialii [W]

[K] Kepookalani + **Alapaiwahine** [W]

[K] **Kamanawa** + Kamokuiki [W]

[K] **Kapaakea** + Keohokalole [W]

David Kalakaua
+
Kapiolani

Miriam Likelike
+
Archibald Cleghorn

Liliuokalani
+
John Owen Dominis

David Kawananakoa

Jonah Kuhio Kalanianaole

Victoria Kaiulani

Lydia Aholo

Joseph Aea

John Aimoku Dominis

ON HER MOTHER'S (KEOHOKALOLE) SIDE

[K] Ahu a I. + **Umiulaikaahumanu** [W]

[K] **Heulu** + Ikuaana [W]

[K] **Keawe-a-Heulu** + Ululani [W]

[K] Kepookalani + **Keohohiwa** [W]

[K] **Aikanaka** + Kamaeokalani [W]

[K] Kapaakea + **Keohokalole** [W]

David Kalakaua	**Miriam Likelike**	**Liliuokalani**
+	+	+
Kapiolani	Archibald Cleghorn	John Owen Dominis

David Kawananakoa	**Victoria Kaiulani**	Lydia Aholo
Jonah Kuhio Kalanianaole		Joseph Aea
		John Aimoku Dominis

Introduction

Starting in the mid-nineteenth century, when photography was a newly popularized technology, calling cards called *carte de visite* became very popular. Left behind after paying a visit or exchanged when traveling, Lili'uokalani had seven albums of *carte de visite* pictures, their contents collected by her from the 1850s to the 1890s. Many of the pictures in the pages that follow are taken from her collection as are the floral designs used on the cover and in chapter headings.

Lili'uokalani: A Royal Album follows eight decades of a remarkable life, with text and pictures integrated to tell her personal story and that of the times in which she lived. The quotes that accompany the pictures are taken from *A Queen's Story by Hawaii's Queen* penned by Lili'uokalani as a memoir written to establish the justice of her cause fighting annexation.

These were transformative decades in which the child born as Lili'u Loloku Walania Wewehi Kamaka'eha became Lydia Pākī, Mrs. John Dominis, Queen Lili'uokalani, and in her later life simply the Queen. I have used the name appropriate to the chapter's time frame. She is Lydia Pākī in the 1840s and 1850s, Lydia Dominis in the 1860s and 1870s until she is named heir to the throne in 1877, and is thereafter Lili'uokalani.

I have selected pictures that follow her from teenager to septuagenarian, supplemented by images of the people and events impacting her life. Many are portraits, allowing a revealing face-to-face look. Since many pictures are undated, the circa symbol provides a frame of reference defined by photo technique, clothing, hair styles, and other visual clues and are close to the time frame they represent.

The story of Lili'uokalani's life—both interesting and intriguing, privileged and at times tragic—is ultimately inspiring. Well-educated and observant, she would outlive all of her contemporaries, isolated by the loss of family and friends, fast-changing times, her royal status, and history's on-coming tide. Serious-minded and competent, she was justified in her concerns for her people and understood that only a strong monarch could protect them from further marginalization. She fought as best she could, without the political or martial resources to resist. Yet she survived to become a symbol of resistance that makes her a living presence today.

Culturally she was a hybrid, as were all of the royal children of her generation. Hawaiian by blood and by what she had learned of her culture from those with memories of the days of old, she was taught within the stern and demanding framework of missionary Christianity. She had a love of learning and a probing mind that pushed beyond dogmatic views to the heart of Christ's message, benefitting from the power of faith. And she was a woman of creative talent, a poet, and composer of renown.

Her message to her people was 'Onipa'a…remain steadfast, a call she came to represent. Now, a century since her passing, her voice remains strong, her music and lyrics still inspire with their message of faith, love, beauty, and reconciliation. And thanks to the Queen Lili'uokalani Trust, her estate supports the children she loved—a valuable part of her enduring legacy.

CHAPTER ONE
SEPTEMBER 2, 1838

An Aliʻi is Born

SEPTEMBER 2, 1838. The past lingers, but it is being overtaken by foreign influences. It is now sixty years since Cook's fateful landfall—long enough to put to rest the ways of old. Missionary influence prevails with a large percentage of Hawaiians, including most of the chiefs attending the birth of a newborn, having converted to Congregationalist Christianity. Despite the rejection of the old gods, the chiefs are still held in high esteem, their authority and prerogatives preserved. Loved and indulged, they are seen as providing continuity in a fast-changing world.

The growing number of whale ships making port calls each year, creating business opportunities for an increasing population of expatriate Americans and Europeans, heightens American influence. The Native population is in decline, decimated by a range of infectious diseases introduced by outsiders and against which the Hawaiians have no immunity. Measles and influenza prove fatal to tens of thousands in recurring epidemics.

On the morning of September 2, the newborn is one of only 120,000 Hawaiians, far below Cook's estimate of 250,000 islanders in 1778. The child born that morning will be one of a handful of royal children of her generation to survive. Of ten siblings only she, her older brother, David Kalākaua, and her younger sister, Miriam Likelike, will survive to adulthood. Many couples were childless due to infertility or offspring lost to disease.

Cries of the newborn emanate from the home of high chief ʻAikanaka, the newborn's grandfather and commander of the adjacent gun battery atop Puowaina, the "Hill of Sacrifice," that will later come to be called Punchbowl. The king's royal compound is nearby, confirming close ties between the two families.

A rainbow appears overhead in a clear sky, an omen announcing the birth of an aliʻi. The newborn, wrapped in the softest white tapa, is blessed with a genealogy that links her to high-ranking chiefs. Inside the hale, the single room is crowded with those attending the birth, including Kamehameha's daughter, Kīnaʻu, who has been given the honor of naming the infant, again acknowledging close family ties.

Lili'u's link to the Kamehamehas goes back generations, to a grandfather allied with Kamehameha in the civil wars of the 1780s. On her mother's side, she is descended from Keawe-a-Heulu, first cousin to Kamehameha's father. Intermarriage between chiefly families, designed to secure offspring of the highest mana, or spiritual power, occurred in each generation, therefore chiefly families shared many common ancestors. Her lineage would one day secure her family the throne.

Names are created for each child, carefully selected for their meaning, either literal or symbolic. Kīna'u, afflicted with an eye infection, names the newborn Lili'u Loloku Walania Wewehi Kamaka'eha, translating broadly as "the tearful, painful smarting of a sore eye." Shortly after Lili'u's birth, Kīna'u gives birth to a daughter, Kamāmalu. The two infants are nursed by the same nursemaid and are bonded as children of the same milk. Soon after her birth, Lili'u and Kamāmalu are baptized—Lili'u as Lydia, Kamāmalu as Victoria.

Kīna'u is not the only link to the Kamehamehas. In keeping with tradition, Lili'u has been promised to Abner Pākī and his wife, Konia, a granddaughter of Kamehameha I. She is now called Lydia Pākī. As their hānai child, she is a genealogical member of her adopted family. Pākī and Konia already have a daughter, Bernice Pauahi. Though promised as hānai, Kīna'u's death in April of 1839 returns Pauahi to her birth parents soon after Lili'u is born. Seven years her senior, the newborn will come to admire and love her older sister, sharing a relationship that is somewhat more formal than warm, with Lydia seeing her as a role model of Victorian rectitude and womanhood.

The Kingdom of Hawai'i is on the verge of transformative changes. As had his father, Kamehameha III has taken foreigners as advisors to help him navigate Hawai'i's increasingly complicated relationship with powerful countries jockeying for influence, each seeking to take advantage of Hawai'i's strategic mid-Pacific location. The most influential had arrived as missionaries and now serve in ministerial and advisory roles to the king. With their help, he has decided to modernize his kingdom.

Opposite page: Lili'u was born in the hale of her grandfather 'Aikanaka (c. 1780-1837) at the base of Puowaina (Punchbowl).

The year of her birth, Kamehameha III, in the thirteenth year of his twenty-nine-year-long reign, has created a preliminary constitution for his kingdom that is formally implemented by royal proclamation in 1840. In a process designed to secure recognition of Hawai'i's legitimacy as an independent nation the royal government was transformed into a constitutional monarchy.

Nurtured by loving parents in a happy and prosperous home, Lydia Pākī thrives. As the last year of the 1830s plays out, Kamehameha's royal court moves to Lahaina which, after Honolulu, is Hawai'i's second busiest port-of-call. Pākī, an influential advisor to the king and successful trader also moves to Maui with his family.

"*My father's name was Kapaakea, and my mother was Keohokalole; the latter was one of the fifteen counsellors of the king, Kamehameha III... My great-grandfather Keawe-a-Heulu, the founder of the dynasty of the Kamehamehas, and Keoua, father of Kamehameha I, were own cousins and my great grandaunt was the celebrated Queen Kapiolani, one of the first converts to Christianity (whose actions) broke forever the power of Pele...over the hearts of her people.*"

"$\mathcal{I}$*knew no other father or mother than my foster-parents, no other sister than Bernice. I used to climb up on the knees of Pākī, put my arms around his neck, kiss him, and he caressed me as a father would his child; while on the contrary, when I met my own parents, it was … always with the demeanor I would have shown to any strangers who had noticed me. My own father and mother had other children…most of them being adopted into other chiefly families; and although I knew that these were my own brothers and sisters, yet we met throughout my younger life as though we had not known our common parentage."*

Above: Highborn and influential, Lydia's parents were married in 1828 when both were twenty in what was one of the first Christian marriages in Hawai'i. Pākī was both a successful trader and an advisor to the king.

Opposite page: Lili'u's birth parents, Keohokālole (1816-1869) and Kapa'akea (1815-1866).

"*Kinau always preferred to take me into her arms to nurse, and would hand her own child* [Victoria Kamāmalu] *to the woman attendant who was there for that purpose. She frequently declared…that a bond of the closest friendship must always exist between her own baby girl and myself as aikane or foster-children of the same mother…just as if I had been her own child.*"

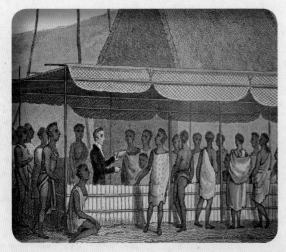

Missionaries and whalers opened Hawai'i to the sacred, the profane, and American influence, although in 1838, the British and the French seemed positioned to secure predominance.

Opposite page
Top left: Lili'u's nursemaid, Hulipahu. Ali'i children were often cared for by family retainers. **right:** Victoria Kamāmalu. **Bottom:** Kīna'u returns from church, while French sailors look on, with Honolulu as a backdrop.

Right: Kamehameha III and Queen Kalama. When Lili'u was born, Kamehameha III was in the thirteenth year of his kingdom-changing, twenty-nine-year reign.

Above, top left: John Papa ʻIʻi (1800-1870). Born on Oʻahu, he was raised to serve in the royal court. He was renowned for his knowledge and respect for the ways of old. He was Kamehameha II's childhood friend and served as an influential advisor to Kamehameha III. top right: The Rev. William Richards (1793-1847) settled in Hawaiʻi in 1825. He helped create a written version of the Hawaiian language and translated the Bible into Hawaiian. In 1838 he resigned from the Mission and became an advisor to Kamehameha III, involved in the creation of Hawaiʻi as a constitutional monarchy and laying the groundwork for the Great Mahele. In 1842 he was named special envoy of the kingdom negotiating with foreign governments to secure guarantees of Hawaiian independence. Above: The first ʻIolani Palace had been built by Mataio Kekuanaoʻa for his daughter Victoria Kamāmalu, but Kamehameha III bought it for an official royal residence.

By 1838, hundreds of whalers were making Honolulu and Lahaina two of the busiest ports in the Pacific. Business prospects drew numbers of foreigners as well. David Malo saw the dangers this presented.

"*If a big wave comes in large fishes will come from the dark ocean which you never saw before, and when they see the small fishes they will eat them up; such also is the case with large animals, they will prey on the smaller ones; the ships of the whitemen have come, and smart people have arrived from the Great Countries which you have never seen before, they know our people are few in number and living in a small country; they will eat us up, such has always been the case with large countries, the small ones have been gobbled up.*"

—DAVID MALO

Above right: David Malo (1793-1853) documented Hawaiʻi's oral history and traditions. He was a student in the first class at Lahainaluna School under William Richards. Malo's quote proved prophetic as Western influence came to prevail. **left:** Samuel Kamakau (1815-1876) wrote of Hawaiian traditions and customs, proving an invaluable resource on the Hawaiian past, also serving in the legislature.

"I was a studious girl; and the acquisition of knowledge has been a passion with me my whole life..."

CHAPTER TWO
THE 1840s

Childhood Days

YDIA SPENT MOST OF HER FIRST FIVE YEARS ON MAUI. Life was slower paced than in Honolulu, but Lahaina was also a busy port hosting whalers and seamen by the hundreds, providing the grog shops and women that sailors craved after long months at sea. The presence of the royal court had a sobering impact, as did a strong missionary presence, with Lahainaluna School and its print house providing a modern education for the growing Christian population.

In 1843 when she was four-and-a-half, Lydia was sent to O'ahu to attend the Chiefs' Children's School as a boarding student. She and Victoria Kamāmalu were the two youngest of thirteen royal students that included future kings Kamehameha IV and V, Lunalilo, and Lydia's brother, David Kalākaua.

Two years her senior, raised in different families and gravitating toward different playmates at school, Kalākaua and Lydia barely knew one another. That would change to sincere affection as bonds of music, kinship, and royal responsibilities opened the door to a close, although sometimes contentious, relationship.

The Chiefs' Children's School had opened in 1839 at the request of the Council of Chiefs who realized the necessity of educating the next generation in the ways of a fast-changing world.

Lahaina, c. 1840. It was here that Lydia Pākī would spend her first few years.

"*At the age of four years I was sent to what was then known as the Royal School, because its pupils were exclusively persons whose claim to the throne were acknowledged…It was a boarding-school, the pupils being allowed to return to their homes on vacation time as well as for an occasional Sunday. The family life was made agreeable to us, our instructors were especially particular to teach us the English language; but when I recall the instances in which we were sent hungry to bed, it seems to me that they failed to remember that we were growing children…we were sometimes ingenious, if not overly honest, in our search for food. As a last resort we were not above searching the gardens for any succulent root or leaf…*"

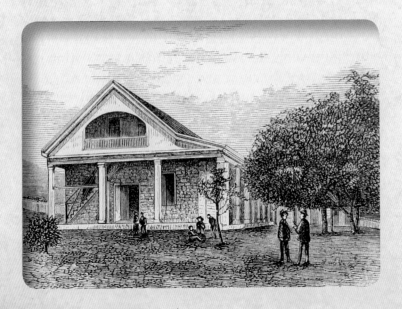

"*I can recall that I was carried there on the shoulders of a tall, stout, very large woman whose name was Kaikai. As she put me down…I shrank from its doors…Crying bitterly I turned to my faithful attendant, clasping her with my arms and clinging closely to her neck. She tenderly expostulated with me; and as the children, moved by curiosity to meet the new-comer, crowded about me, I was soon attracted by their friendly faces and my fears began to vanish, and comforted and consoled, I soon found myself at home amongst my playmates.*"

Amos Starr Cooke & Juliette Montague Cooke with two of their children, who were also students at the school. **Opposite page:** The Chiefs' Children's School or Royal School in a sketch from the 1840s.

Amos Starr Cooke and his wife, Juliette, having recently arrived with the Seventh Company of American missionaries, opened the school on land granted by the king whose hānai children, Alexander Liholiho, Kauikeauoli, and Victoria Kamāmalu were enrolled.

The Cookes, austere in tastes and habits, were demanding of their entitled "scholars," as they called their royal charges. Held in awe by the Hawaiians and used to respect and deference due to their high rank, the boys chafed under the rigidity, conformity, and self-restraint that the Cookes expected of themselves and others.

The girls were more compliant, most particularly Bernice Pauahi (Juliette Cooke's favorite), Kamehameha's great-granddaughter molded into a model of Victorian womanhood and Christian virtue. Soft-spoken and emotionally restrained, she was a role model in the process of self-perfection that would mark Lydia's life.

Bernice Pauahi, c. 1848

Lydia was more free-spirited and independent than her sister, although she too absorbed the standards that were part of her missionary education. Also trained in the ways of her people, there was a divide between the traditions and instincts of her Hawaiian ancestry and the rigid, missionary imprint of behavior and belief, power versus humility, revenge versus forgiveness, sexual freedom with sexual repression, old gods and new gods. There was much to consider straddling this cultural divide. With an ongoing pursuit of knowledge and open-minded inquiry, she sought the

"She was one of the most beautiful girls I ever saw; the vision of her loveliness at the time can never be effaced from remembrance. [She was] as good as she was beautiful."

spiritual answers that mattered to her, experimenting with mysticism and embracing more than one religion as the decades accumulated.

Her sense of her childhood was mostly positive. Joyful in her family life, playful and studious, she proved an excellent student, proficient in English and Hawaiian, and excelling in all her studies.

The 1840s would prove a challenging decade for Hawai'i, with the kingdom in the crosshairs of colonial powers—most notably the French and the British who, self-righteously declaring their honor at stake, secured financial and political objectives using threats and guns. The French had already taken over Tahiti and the Marquesas and the British controlled New Zealand and scattered outposts elsewhere in the Pacific. Strategically located, Hawai'i was the ultimate prize. None of the contending powers, which included the United States, was willing to see Hawai'i fall to its rivals.

Since the early 1800s, Britain, France, and the U.S. had naval ships traversing the Pacific. Resident commissioners represented each government in Honolulu. Keeping a wary eye on one another, they also made demands of the royal government ensnaring the kingdom into protracted and costly disputes.

As his father had done, Kamehameha III sought the advice of foreigners, including those who left both the American and British Missions to serve the Crown. Their influence would be felt in the transformative events that marked Lydia's childhood years.

In 1840, Kamehameha III, seeking to affirm Hawai'i's national identity, promulgated an enlightened constitution inspired by British and American models of constitutional government that defined the rights of chiefs and commoners, granted religious freedom, established the rule of law, and created a legislative and judicial balance to royal power.

In 1842, with a constitutional monarchy established, the king sent emissaries to Europe and the United States successfully securing treaties and affirming Hawai'i's independence. Such efforts would not prove foolproof, however, as Lydia and her royal classmates soon discovered.

Left: British troops landed and removed the king, establishing an unofficial protectorate of the kingdom. The king was advised by William Richards, Gerrit Judd and Robert Wyllie—three key foreign-born members of his Privy Council. Richards was then sent to London to negotiate a settlement which resulted in sending Admiral Thomas (left) to Hawai'i, where he restored Kamehameha III to the throne. Lydia saw both the king's humiliation and the restoration ceremony, hoping when she was queen, that a similar outcome would follow her overthrow.

Below: Emma Rooke (1836-1885) and her uncle Keoni Ana (1810-1857), c. 1848. Seven years later, she would become queen.

In 1843, a British naval force landed at Honolulu under the command of George Paulet who'd been authorized to investigate claims that the rights of British citizens in the kingdom were being compromised. Without further authorization from the British government, Paulet proved arrogant and willing to use force, as stated in a letter alerting the captain of the USS *Boston* at anchor in Honolulu harbor.

"Sir, I have the honour to notify you that Her Britannic Majesty's Ship Carysfort, under my command, will be prepared to make an immediate attack upon this town [Honolulu], *at 4 o'clock P.M. to-morrow, (Saturday) in the event of the demands now forwarded by me to the King of these Islands not being complied with by that time."*

The threatened attack followed, with the king deposed and Hawai'i declared a British protectorate by Paulet. Although not quite five, Lydia experienced the sense of uncertainty and turmoil Paulet's actions had caused, with the king humiliated and Hawai'i's independence undone.

She was with her classmates five months later, assembled on a grassy plain to the east of the city (today Thomas Square), as the British flag was lowered, the Hawaiian flag—complete with Union Jack—was raised, and the king restored to his throne. "Ua Mau ke Ea o ka 'Āina i ka Pono," the king had proclaimed…The Life of the Land is Perpetuated in Righteousness, honoring the justice of the outcome. One day fifty years in the future, as a deposed queen, Lili'uokalani would hope for a similar restoration, to no avail.

Lydia was an intelligent and impressionable eleven-year-old in 1849 when she saw the French impose their will, demanding trade concessions for French goods and further securing the rights of Catholic missionaries. Violence was again the method of coercion, with harborside Fort Kekuanohu, built by Kamehameha in 1816, shelled. The fort's defensive cannon were dismantled and the town sacked before concessions and a large indemnity were extorted from the kingdom under threat of further violence. The king was again humbled and the kingdom was forced to surrender to secure a French withdrawal. Such were the lessons of history that would provide Lydia with painful memories and a strong political will.

By the end of the decade, the process of Westernization took aim at land ownership. Hawai'i's communally held lands, distributed by a hierarchy of ali'i administrators, was replaced by private, deeded ownership in a process called the Great Mahele (Division).

Initially, lands were granted to the king and to chiefs with ancestral claims. Lydia would inherit family holdings on

Victoria Kamāmalu with her birth father, Mataio Kekuanao'a, c. 1848.

Timothy Haʻalilio (1808-1844) would travel to Europe and New England where he became fluent in English. Kamehameha III appointed him as an ambassador for the kingdom in 1842.

"Haalilio was a man of intelligence, of good judgement, of pleasing manners, and respectable business habits. ...few public officers possess integrity more trustworthy."

—HIRAM BINGHAM

Oʻahu and the Island of Hawaiʻi under the Mahele.

In 1850, mahele grants were extended to commoners who could claim three-acre lots. Of greater consequence, the right to own land was also granted to non-Natives including non-citizens. It proved to be a policy with fateful consequences, weakening communal bonds while alienating thousands of acres from Native ownership. While the Hawaiian population continued its free fall decline, the number of ambitious foreigners residing in the kingdom was on the rise. That included missionary offspring who retained strong emotional, philosophical, and educational ties to the United States. As the Native population declined, foreigners and non-Native citizens bought land that was lost by Hawaiian families due to death and unpaid taxes.

In the decades that followed, tens of thousands of acres were also sold by cash-poor royals. Land sales continued to increase in the decades that followed as prospering sugar plantations sought additional acreage. By the late 1850s, with whaling in steep decline, sugar would become the foundation of the kingdom's economy. With that came ever-greater integration of the Hawaiian and American economies.

Of more immediate concern was the devastation wrought by ongoing epidemics. Lydia's schoolmates had been lost in the smallpox epidemic of 1843 that took thousands of lives. Lydia was personally impacted by the loss of her four-year-old sister, Kaʻiminaʻauao, in the measles epidemic of 1848 followed in 1852 by the loss of her brother James Kaliokalani at age sixteen. With each death the Hawaiian gene pool was being diminished. Seeming infertility, with many couples remaining childless, compounded the problem. Large numbers of families were dying out and talk of the end of the Hawaiians as a people appeared in newspapers and was discussed in the community at large. She later recalled efforts at halting the spread of illness eliminating the traditional lengthy mourning period that Hawaiian tradition required:

> *"…relatives and companions of my youth died and were buried on the same day, the coffin of the last-named resting on that of the others."*

The measles epidemic of 1848 led to the closing of the Chiefs' Children's School. That was a happy occasion for Lydia, who was restored to the loving family of her earliest years, with the royal court, including Pākī and Konia, once again based in Honolulu. She continued her formal education at the new Royal School run by Reverend Edgar Beckwith with typical missionary rigor until she was seventeen.

Lydia's home life was happy, a place where aspects of the Hawaiian past preserved by Pākī and Konia, nutured her Hawaiian soul. Her inquisitive nature, tamed by

Gerrit Judd accompanied the princes Lot Kapuāiwa (left) and Alexander Liholiho (right) on a year-long trip to the U.S. and Europe in 1849-50, seeking to educate them and present the future kings to the Euro-American political establishment. Judd, who arrived in Hawaiʻi with the Third Company of American Missionaries in 1827, left the Mission in 1842 to became a trusted advisor and government minister to Kamehameha III. Later, Liliʻuokalani would disparage Judd as an example of missionary influence that worked against the best interests of the Hawaiians.

missionary influence, was enhanced by contacts with the outside world, for in addition to his government posts, Pākī was a businessman with wide-ranging connections. He played host to an array of visitors from ship captains to naval officers to traders en route to and from Asia.

For the next five years, Haleakalā, Pākī's sheltered house, with its wide verandas and landscaped yard on the outskirts of Honolulu, was home. Having mastered reading, spelling, penmanship, arithmetic, geometry, algebra, physics, geography, history, bookkeeping, singing, and English composition, Lydia was already an impressive young woman. As the 1840s drew to an end Lydia Pākī entered her teenage years.

Above: Honolulu Harbor, c. 1845. **Below:** In 1849, French naval forces bombarded Kekuanohu Fort built by Kamehameha in 1816, destroying its cannon and threatening further violence unless its demands were met. For the second time Lydia, an impressionable eleven-year-old, would see the king humiliated and Hawaiʻi's autonomy compromised by foreign intervention. The fort was not restored, with the interior thereafter used as a parade ground.

"*The age of Kamehameha III was that of progress and of liberty, of schools and civilization. He gave us a constitution and gave us fixed laws; he secured the people in the title to their lands, and removed the last chain of oppression…He was a great national benefactor, and has left the impress of his mild and amiable disposition on the age for which he was born.*"

—ALEXANDER LIHOLIHO, KAMEHAMEHA III'S FUNERAL ORATION

Above, top left: Kauikeaouli in 1825. *Honolulu Museum of Art* top right: As King Kamehameha III (1813-1854) c. 1845. *Bishop Museum* bottom left: Kamehameha III (c. 1849) was aged by the pressures of kingship in unsettled times, relying on both Lydia's birth father, Mataio Kekuanaoʻa, and her hānai father, Abner Pākī, as advisors and Ministers. bottom right: Queen Kalama, consort of Kamehameha III. Having lost two sons in infancy, she served as mother to her three hānai children.

Dressed in black satin at the start of her teenage years, c. 1851.

CHAPTER THREE
THE 1850s

The Teenage Years

ROM THE START, THE 1850s WOULD BE A DECADE OF CHANGE FOR LYDIA PĀKĪ. In 1850, she served in the wedding party of her sister, Bernice. Her parents objected, for Bernice had been promised at birth as a bride to her cousin, Lot Kamehameha, a partner suited to her own high status. The breach seemed permanent, with Pākī transferring Bernice's inheritance to Lydia, only to take it back entirely when the breach between parents and daughter was resolved. Lydia had sought redress, but the court decided against her, declaring that her hānai status was not legally valid. Bernice had selected a handsome, respected, American-born businessman named Charles Reed Bishop. She was eighteen and he was twenty-eight. The seed of romance had been sown in teenage Lydia's mind.

Haleakalā was a landscaped oasis, located not far from where King and Bishop streets now intersect, in close proximity to the king's court where Pākī served on the Privy Council and as the King's Chamberlain. It was a home open to the outside world, although that changed after Pākī's death in 1855 and yet again in 1857 with Konia's passing when Lydia was eighteen. The Bishops stepped in, making a home for Lydia at Haleakalā, which Bernice had inherited, encouraging in her the social graces suited to the culturally-hybrid world in which they socialized.

The economic trends of the 1840s continued into the 1850s, with whaling still booming and sugar on the rise, creating opportunities for men like James Campbell, an adventurous Scotsman who reached Hawai'i in 1847. Married into Hawaiian royalty, he became one of the richest and most influential men in the kingdom. Others, like James Castle and Samuel Cooke, left the Mission to open a dry goods store that grew into one of Hawai'i's largest businesses. Business meant banking, with Charles Bishop opening Bishop Bank in 1858 to facilitate the loans that financed the rapid

Above left: With her sister, Bernice Pauahi, c. 1857, both in Victorian finery. Pauahi proved a powerful role model for Lydia. Pākī and Konia had arranged for Pauahi to marry Lot Kamehameha, but lovestruck, she refused, instead marrying Charles Reed Bishop. The simple wedding ceremony was held at the home of missionary Hiram Bingham. Neither Pākī nor Konia attended, but Lydia was in the wedding party. **right:** Bernice as a young bride with her groom, Charles Reed Bishop, 1851. **Below:** Honolulu at the start of the 1850s. One of the earliest views of the city by photographer Hugo Stangenwald.

expansion and technological advances impacting plantation sugar, which was almost entirely owned by non-Native entrepreneurs. By the end of the decade, sugar was already providing revenues equal to those generated by servicing ships. Whaling was soon eclipsed by the discovery of oil in Pennsylvania in 1859, with kerosene replacing whale oil in American homes. Whaling's precipitous decline in the 1860s was matched by sugar's rise.

Born in 1834, Kamehameha IV was of Lydia's generation and had experienced the same transformative events of the 1840s. He realized the need for advisors who could effectively negotiate with covetous Euro-American powers, with foreign-born advisors and ministers dominating the new king's government and Privy Council. Treaties with the great powers were signed, reformulated, and resigned—an indication of the sensitive balance of power that made for peaceful times.

At twenty-one as the decade ended, Lydia Pākī was a very eligible young woman. William Lunalilo, a cousin to the Kamehamehas and later king, was a suitor seeking Lydia's hand in marriage despite a prior engagement to Victoria Kamāmalu. Lydia ultimately rejected his offer, leaving only Lot Kamehameha as a possible partner. He had been promised to Bernice Pauahi at birth, but he was not her choice and while Lydia was considered, he remained a bachelor. With few others of adequate rank in the Hawaiian community to consider and with Bernice as an example, Lydia ultimately accepted the proposal of a foreign-born suitor.

The Bishops provided a comfortable home for Lydia with the continuity of life at Haleakalā easing the painful loss of Pākī and Konia. A high-spirited young woman, Lydia enjoyed the social whirl that included the royal and non-Native elite—young entrepreneurial men who found a congenial home in the kingdom and in the hearts, however misplaced, of high-born Native women. There were late night balls and parties shared with family and friends, the women dressed in the height of Victorian fashion in dresses imported from Paris, San Francisco, and New York.

Trained to be a Victorian woman of quality—knowledgeable and conversant in many subjects, Lydia also received piano lessons and was self-taught on the 'ukulele and other instruments. She was versed in history,

"*He then asked me in the presence of my attendants why we shouldn't get married. There was an aged native preacher…who at once offered to perform the ceremony. But having heard that the prince was engaged to his cousin Victoria* [Kamāmalu] *I did not consider it right to marry him, on the impulse of the moment…he supposed that I had rejected his proposal; but on hearing my explanation* [a letter sent on a ship that was lost at sea] *he again renewed his offer, and we became engaged.*"

Above: Lydia, c. 1858, at about the time she was temporarily engaged to William Lunalilo (1835-1875), later Hawai'i's sixth king. **Right:** William Lunalilo proposed to Lydia in 1857 when she was nineteen and he was twenty-two, but miscommunication, uncertainty, and the royal disapproval of Kamehameha III, ended the engagement. Lunalilo remained a bachelor.

Opposite page
Haleakalā, the family home Pākī built for Konia, Bernice, and Lydia. She would live there throughout the 1850s.

literature, and mathematics, and was adept at English and Hawaiian, making her Hawaiʻi's most capable linguist. These talents also made her one of Hawaiʻi's most renowned lyric composers.

Literacy proved a valuable extension of the missionary experience, particularly for a self-motivated, retentive student like Lydia. Literacy was made possible by a missionary-crafted alphabet brought to Hawaiʻi from Tahiti and adapted to Hawaiian tonalities. To the missionaries, literacy meant both the Bible and teaching practical skills suited to the Christian utopia they had in mind. By the 1850s, the Hawaiians were among the most literate people in the world.

Kamehameha IV and Queen Emma made health issues the hallmark of their reign. Failing to receive legislative support for a healthcare plan that addressed the epidemics decimating the kingdom's Native population, the King, Queen, Lydia, and other royals personally contributed to, and solicited funds for, what was initially a maternity hospital that took aim at the high death rate of Hawaiian newborns. The nearly $15,000 collected was used to found the Queen's Hospital in 1859.

In 1854, the nation was shaken by the death of Kamehameha III. In the twenty-ninth year of his transformative reign, he left the kingdom in the hands of his ill-prepared twenty-year-old hānai son, Alexander Liholiho.

The well-liked new king's reign as Kamehameha IV began in January of 1855. The following year he married the equally well-liked Emma Rooke in a ceremony with Lydia in the wedding party. Two years later, a joyful nation heard of the birth of Albert, Prince of Hawaiʻi, or Ka Haku O Hawaiʻi (Lord of Hawaiʻi) as his adoring subjects spoke of him. It was a short-lived time of joy and hope for the dynasty's future.

" *Some* of those interested in the genealogies of the historic families of the Hawaiian chiefs, on hearing of this intended marriage, went to the king and begged him to change his mind. "And why should I?" asked Liholiho. "Because, Your Majesty, there is no other chief equal to you in birth and rank but the adopted daughter of Paki." The king took offense…and dismissed the objectors from his presence. "

Above: Kamehameha IV. At age twenty-one Emma Rooke was married to Kamehameha IV then in the second year of his nine-year-long reign. **Right:** Their royal offspring, Albert, Prince of Hawaiʻi, was a bright and playful boy adored by the nation. Born in 1858, he was the first royal child of his generation and a sign of hope for the future.

Opposite page: The wedding of Kamehameha IV and Emma Rooke excited the hopes of the nation. Also in the scene are Mataio Kekuanaoʻa, the king's birth father, Victoria Kamāmalu to the far right, and Kalākaua and Kapiʻolani midway up the stairs. Lot Kamehameha and Bernice are conversing at the top of the stairs, with an admirer glancing upward at Lydia Pākī who stands alone at the balustrade.

Pākī (above left) died in 1855 and Konia (above right) died in 1857 leaving Lydia in the care of the Bishops. **Below left:** Lydia's world would expand to include her sister, Miriam Likelike (1851-1887), and brother, Leleiōhoku (1854-1877), (right) who was taken as hānai by Kamehameha's great-granddaughter, Ruth Keʻelikōlani, further strengthening ties between the Kamehamehas and the Kalākauas.

Liliʻuokalani in a fancy gingham dress, c. 1859. She and her fellow royals ordered clothes from San Francisco, New York, London, and Paris. By the 1880s, Victorian fashion, with its bustles and bows, would end the reign of missionary-inspired simplicity.

Robert Wyllie (1798-1865) arrived in Hawaiʻi after a life of adventure when he was forty-five. Within a year he was Kamehameha III's Minister of Foreign Affairs, a position he held for twenty years, negotiating for the kingdom with covetous foreign powers. He acted as a British balance to Gerrit Judd's commanding influence. Working on behalf of the Royal Government, Wyllie traveled widely and successfully negotiated treaties with the United States, Great Britain, France, and Denmark. He was a founding member of the Hawaiʻi Agricultural Society and initiated the collections of the Hawaiʻi Archives.

Whaling remained the backbone of the economy, but that would change by the end of the decade when petroleum, discovered in Pennsylvania in 1859, replaced whale oil as a source of heat and light. Sugar was waiting in the wings as an alternative, with plantations expanding. The Hawaiian Agricultural Society was created in 1855 to promote scientific agriculture and commerce.

Lydia Pākī in a stylish gown. She appreciated high fashion and often dressed the part. In a picture taken at the Chase studio in Honolulu, a young woman emerges from her teenage years. As 1859 drew to a close, she was ready for marriage with the Bishops ready to provide a helping hand.

Lydia Dominis, c. 1865.

CHAPTER FOUR
THE 1860S

Mrs. John Dominis

ONE SEPTEMBER 16, 1862, TWO WEEKS AFTER HER TWENTY-FOURTH BIRTHDAY, Lydia Pākī married John Owen Dominis with the Bishops as her sponsors. Well-liked in the expatriate community, Dominis proved to be a loyal, well-informed advisor, although an emotionally inappropriate partner, dominated by a mother who held on to her son to compensate for the loss of her sea-captain husband and two daughters. In 1846, when John Owen was fourteen, his father set sail for the Orient and was lost at sea, leaving behind a grieving widow and a son who catered to his mother's demands and expectations. With Christian charity, Lydia sought to accept the consequences of her husband's attachment to a mother who saw her as competition for John Owen's affections and who had scant regard for Lydia's high rank. She showed her displeasure by refusing to attend their wedding.

Dominis Sr. had completed a home for his family that was one of the finest in the city, situated within a short walk of the first ʻIolani Palace. Following the wedding, Lydia Dominis moved from Haleakalā to Washington Place, as the Dominis' residence came to be called. She was not made to feel welcome, and began to spend time in her homes in Waikīkī and Kapālama.

The wedding had been postponed due to the death of the Prince of Hawaiʻi at the age of four. Adored by the nation and a symbol of the future, he had taken sick with what was likely appendicitis and died several days later on August 27, 1862. The loss of his son, and of a friend he'd critically injured in a moment of anger, left the king beyond comfort and the nation with a despairing sense of loss. The young prince's passing proved more impactful than the saddened young bride understood. No other royal Kamehameha heir of that generation would follow Albert.

Within fifteen months of Prince Albert's passing, the King would also be gone, succumbing to depression and chronic asthma at the age of twenty-nine.

"*...Slowly* [Mary Dominis] *was compelled to recognize the truth* [of irreparable loss] *so many sailors' wives are constantly learning... For this reason she clung with tenacity to the affection and constant attentions of her son, and no man could have been more devoted than was General Dominis to his mother... As she felt that no one should step between her and her child, naturally I, as her son's wife, was considered an intruder; and I was forced to realize this from the beginning.*"

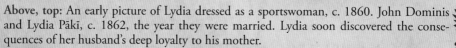
Above, top: An early picture of Lydia dressed as a sportswoman, c. 1860. John Dominis and Lydia Pākī, c. 1862, the year they were married. Lydia soon discovered the consequences of her husband's deep loyalty to his mother.

Lot Kamehameha assumed the title of Kamehameha V following his brother's death. He was well-prepared to rule, having served in a number of key government positions during his brother's reign. Strong-willed, physically imposing, and regally self-empowered, he unilaterally promulgated a new constitution for the kingdom in 1864 when confronted by inaction by the legislature. The new constitution was designed to restore powers to the throne, the king understanding that a strong monarchy was the best guarantor of Hawaiian independence. Kamehameha V effectively governed the kingdom, providing a sense of stability and chiefly authority that Lydia admired. Lili'uokalani would see in his actions, and those of his predecessors, precedents that allowed for monarchical intervention. Impressed by his resolve, Lydia ultimately would make his slogan, 'Onipa'a—to remain steadfast and unyielding in principle, her own as well.

Kamehameha V was called "…the last of the great chiefs of the olden times." Lydia composed music on royal request, including the ballad *Ka Lāhui O Hawai'i,* which served as Hawai'i's national anthem until replaced by *Hawai'i Pono'ī,* which was composed by David Kalākaua. She supported his efforts at preserving Hawai'i as a Polynesian kingdom and praised the constitution of 1864 which restored royal power.

"*An unusually sweet child, gentle and gentlemanly in his manners, bright and precocious and of a most happy, serene temperament.*"

—FREDERICK ALLEN, A CHILDHOOD PLAYMATE OF THE YOUNG PRINCE, DESCRIBING ALBERT

Above: August 27, 1862. Albert Edward Kauikeaouli Leiopapa, Prince of Hawai'i, died, likely of improperly diagnosed appendicitis. The king held himself responsible, having doused his son with cold water prior to the outset of the illness that took his life. In 1863, the twenty-nine-year-old king, prematurely aged and wearied by the demands of kingship, died of acute asthma. *Bishop Museum* **Right:** 1866. Emma in mourning beneath pictures of her lost son and husband. In 1874, following Lunalilo's death she challenged Kalākaua in the election for monarch.

The Queen's Hospital was built near Lili'uokalani's birthplace. When government funds were not forthcoming, the king and queen provided seed money and solicited the funds to build The Queen's Hospital in the 1860s.

A voice upon the prairies,
  A cry of woman's woe
That mingleth with the autumn blast
All fitfully and low;
It is a mother's wailing:
Has earth another tone
Like that with which a mother mourns.
Her lost, her only one?

Above left: Ruth Keʻelikōlani. Having lost two sons, she took Leleiōhoku as her hānai son. right: The youngest of Lydia's siblings, Leleiōhoku, at the age of fifteen. His death in 1877 would position Lydia as heir to the throne. Had he lived and been Keʻelikōlani's heir, he might well have linked the landed wealth of the Kamehamehas and the Crown providing the monarchy with significant financial resources independent of legislative approval.

" *Practice humility…Remember then duty before pleasure.* "

—LYDIA DOMINIS
ADVISES HER YOUNGER SISTER,
MIRIAM LIKELIKE, 1866.

Miriam Likelike, born when Lydia was thirteen, collaborated with Liliʻuokalani on community projects and was also a composer. Despite cautionary precedents, she would marry Scotsman Archibald Cleghorn at age nineteen.

Lydia and John. Miriam Likelike, backed by her husband Archibald Cleghorn, sits beside Lydia. Both women suffered in unhappy marriages with men who personally disregarded their aliʻi status and proved emotionally incompatible.

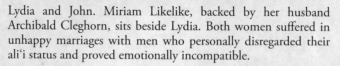

"*In the year 1869 the Duke of Edinburgh, Prince Alfred of England, arrived in the harbor of Honolulu, being in command of Her Britannic Majesty's ship-of-war Galatea…So at his* [Kamehameha V] *specific request I gave a grand luau at my Waikiki residence, to which were invited all those connected with the government, indeed, all the first families of the city, whether of native or foreign birth.*"

The pull of the American economy grew noticeably stronger during the 1860s, with a sugar boom fueled first by the California gold rush and then by the Civil War (1861-1865), which opened the door to Hawaiian sugar when Louisiana sugar was cut off from Union markets.

Above right: The Duke of Edinburgh paid a royal visit in 1870. Eighteen years later, Lydia was seated beside him in Westminster Abbey in celebration of Queen Victoria's Jubilee.

"This country is the king of the sugar world, as far as astonishing productiveness is concerned. The sugar industry…in its importance to America, surpasses them all."

—MARK TWAIN, 1866

Above: Chinese contract laborers in steerage en route to Hawai'i. Below: The growth of sugar plantations meant importing foreign workers.

Acreage in sugar increased dramatically, with the benefits of sugar-fueled prosperity largely bypassing the Hawaiian community, falling instead to a non-Native oligarchy that began asserting political muscle, pressuring the royal government to pursue tariff advantages for Hawaiian sugar entering the United States.

The expansion of plantation agriculture would soon have dramatic demographic implications, with the demand for plantation labor unmet by the diminishing Hawaiian labor pool. The government, increasingly dependent on sugar revenues, began to look beyond Hawai'i for plantation laborers. Initially seeking a kindred people, in the 1860s the government brought in Gilbertese islanders—a Micronesian people who proved unsuited to plantation labor.

China proved a more successful source. Trade ships had long linked Hawai'i to the Orient. By the end of the decade, thousands of Chinese con-

tract laborers had settled in the islands, including many who remained as non-citizen residents after fulfilling their three-to-five year contracts.

Until the end of the decade, the Hawaiians remained the majority in the kingdom. But the growing numbers of foreigners were met by a Hawaiian population in free fall, declining from 70,600 in 1860 to fewer than 60,000 in 1869. And new afflictions were in the offing. Hansen's Disease (leprosy) took its toll with stringently enforced isolation, first in quarantine in Honolulu and then on the isolated Kalawao Peninsula on Moloka'i's rugged north coast.

The health initiative, begun in 1850 when Kamehameha III's Privy Council created the Board of Health and continued by Kamehameha IV and Queen Emma, made some headway with Queen's Hospital up and running by the mid-1860s. But population statistics reveal the complexity of the situation. Death rates were many times that of birth rates with women and the young disproportionally impacted. By the end of the decade there were far more Hawaiian males than females with infertility compounding the problem.

As a young couple linked to both the Hawaiian and expatriate elite, Lydia and John Dominis were an active part of Hawai'i's social scene, although John would often socialize without her—a sign of the emotional distance that would plague her marriage.

Lydia wrote of the elder Mrs. Dominis' controlling ways, against which her husband seemed powerless as he sacrificed his wife's well-being for his mother's. Of a generous and forgiving nature, in keeping with her Christian beliefs, Lydia suffered her mother-in-law's abusive ways. Mary Dominis relented somewhat in old age and remained a part of their lives until she died in 1889.

A well-connected insider, Dominis served in the House of Nobles and was Governor of both O'ahu and Maui when he died in 1891. For Lydia, he was a valuable link to the political realities facing the kingdom. Although she respected his judgment, he was emotionally remote and dismissive of Lydia and her feelings. By the end of the decade, Lydia Dominis started spending more time away from Washington Place, where she did not feel

Above left: Elizabeth Sinclair, originally from New Zealand, bought the island of Niʻihau from Kamehameha V for $10,000—an example of how vast tracts were sold to non-Natives. **right:** James Campbell, c. 1865. Originally from Ireland, he arrived in Hawaiʻi after years of adventurous travel. He became one of the islands' wealthiest planters and married into Hawaiian royalty. **Below:** Kawaiahaʻo Church, c. 1865. Lydia Dominis led the church choir for a number of years, but ultimately became a congregant at several other Christian denominations. She was a sophisticated thinker who received spiritual solace in the power of Christian ideals and Christ's stoic example.

Above, top photo: Looking inland toward Punchbowl. Not far from Haleakalā and Washington Place, 1867. Above: A Vision of Old Hawai'i. The coast near Waikīkī as the 1860s begin.

Left: Lili'uokalani's Waikīkī home, Paoakalani: The Heavenly Perfume.

welcome or at ease, happily enjoying time at her homes in Kapālama and Waikīkī where she had a wonderful ten-acre, beachfront spread.

The kingdom was at peace, having weathered the economic ups and downs of the sugar trade and its ongoing expansion. Lydia was wary, seeing risks in America's economic embrace. By the 1860s, manifest destiny had spanned the North American continent, with Alaska added in 1867. There had already been talk in the American Congress of taking possession of Hawai'i as early as the 1840s without serious action taken. With sugar linking the Hawaiian and American economies the decades old balance of power was now tilting in America's favor.

Lydia was now in her thirties (below), serving as a sisterly advisor to teenage Likelike, with her youngest brother, Leleiōhoku soon to enter his teens. Brother David had married Kapi'olani, who Lydia considered a congenial companion. Lydia organized the Kawaiaha'o Church Choir, finding another outlet for her love of music. Life was full without being too demanding but transformative change was on a not too distant horizon.

❦ — ❦

Lydia Dominis, c. 1872, approaching middle age and a decade that will rede-fine her and transform her life.

CHAPTER FIVE
THE 1870s

Fate Steps In

 YDIA DOMINIS WAS THIRTY-ONE WHEN THE 1870s BEGAN. She was a strong-willed, independent thinker with an observant eye and well-considered opinions. While she was constrained by the more puritanical imprint of missionary propriety, she enjoyed an active social life, with a flair for fashion that freed her of the black, all-covering styles that had prevailed since the missionaries made modesty a hallmark of virtue.

The decade took a somber tone with the death of Kamehameha V on December 11, 1872, his forty-second birthday. Bernice, the highest ranking of the Kamehamehas, was offered the throne by the dying king, but refused the call to duty, too private and apolitical to confidently handle the burdens of power. There are others, she had declared, but in fact there were none.

The Constitution of 1864, which Kamehameha V had promulgated, called for a vote by the legislature should no heir be named. The election pitted William Lunalilo, Lydia's one-time fiancé, against her brother, David Kalākaua. Lunalilo was well liked by the Hawaiians for his unassuming, egalitarian ways, and was accepted as a cousin to the Kamehamehas, though they neither liked nor respected him. The feeling was mutual, Lunalilo selecting a burial site adjacent to Kawaiahaʻo Church rather than the mausoleum at Mauna ʻAla where the Kamehamehas were laid to rest. Thirteen months after taking the throne, Lunalilo died of alcoholism-induced organ failure.

With no heir named, a vote was again held in 1874, with Kalākaua and Dowager Queen Emma as contenders. Emma was one-quarter English. Her grandfather, John Young, had been Kamehameha's military advisor in the civil war that led to his victory. She was the hānai of her aunt and uncle, British physician Thomas Rooke. She was decidedly pro-British and fearful of America's growing influence. She favored the Anglican Church over the

"The throne belongs to Lunalilo; I will not appoint him, because I consider him unworthy of the position. The constitution, in case I make no nomination, provides for the election of the next King; let it be so."

—KAMEHAMEHA V

Above: William Lunalilo, c. 1871. **Right:** John Dominis, 1873 and Lydia Dominis, c. 1877 (below left), renamed Liliʻuokalani after having been declared Kalākaua's heir. John Dominis served as Governor of both Oʻahu and Maui during much of Kalākaua's reign. **Below right:** Dowager Queen Emma was a renowned equestrian. While living a quiet life after the death of her husband and son, by the 1870s she would be ready to resume a public life.

"To the Hawaiian Nation."

"Salutations to You—Whereas His Majesty Lunalilo departed this life at the hour of nine o'clock last night; and by his death the Throne of Hawaii is left vacant, and the nation is without a head or a guide. In this juncture it is proper that we should seek for a Sovereign and Leader, and doing so, follow the course prescribed by Article 22nd of the Constitution. My earnest desire is for the perpetuity of the Crown and the permanent independence of the government and people of Hawaii, on the basis of the equity, liberty, prosperity, progress and protection of the whole people.

It will be remembered that at the time of the election of the late lamented Sovereign, I put forward my own claim to the Throne of our beloved country, on Constitutional grounds — and it is upon those grounds only that I now prefer my claims, and call upon you to listen to my call, and request you to instruct your Representatives to consider, and weigh well, and to regard your choice to elect me, the oldest member of a family high in rank in the country.

Therefore, I, David Kalakaua, cheerfully call upon you, and respectfully ask you to grant me your support."

—D. KALĀKAUA
ʻIOLANI PALACE, FEB. 4, 1874.

Protestant denomination of the mostly American missionaries and had selected Queen Victoria as godmother to her son, Prince Albert. Emma was a congregant at St. Andrews Cathedral, built with support of Kamehameha IV. Later, Lydia abandoned Kawaiahaʻo for St. Andrews as she pursued a spiritual home.

Emma's partisans considered Kalākaua dangerously vulnerable to the demands of the American sugar planters. The campaign became personal, with Lydia unable to forgive Emma for the way she had demeaned her family's pedigree, a slight of significance in the Hawaiian community. Bad

Above, left: Kalākaua in Masonic garb, c. 1878. The king was a committed Mason, as were many of the Americans in the kingdom including John Dominis. right: Queen Kapiʻolani, c. 1877.

Left: Leleiōhoku, already showing a flair for music, had been named Kalākaua's heir in 1874. His passing in 1877 led to Liliʻuokalani's being named Kalākaua's heir.

Above left: While well-suited to Victorian life, Lydia appreciated the simplicity of the Hawaiian lifestyle. **right:** Likelike's baby daughter, Victoria Kaʻiulani, born in 1875 provided new hope for the future.

blood flowed, mostly from Emma's supporters who rioted and killed one of the legislators, throwing him from a second story window when Kalākaua won a convincing victory and was named king. To quell the rioters, Kalākaua requested support from American and British marines anchored offshore. Peace was quickly restored and the naval forces were removed, but the precedent did not sit well with Lydia despite the outcome.

Kalākaua's victory dramatically impacted Lydia Dominis, renamed Liliʻuokalani by Kalākaua when she was titled a princess. To secure his dynasty, Kalākaua immediately chose his brother Leleiōhoku as his heir. Born in 1854, he had been adopted by Kamehameha's great-granddaughter, Ruth Keʻelikōlani, who had lost her husband and two sons to early deaths. Sadly, Leleiōhoku suffered the same fate, dying at twenty-three of rheumatic fever in 1877. With Leleiōhoku's death, Liliʻuokalani was named heir, a position she handled with constitutional diligence and to widespread acclaim. While deferring to Kalākaua as king, she was not afraid to express opposition to policies she thought weakened royal authority, seeing Kamehameha's more autocratic ways as the best defense of the kingdom's independence.

Calling cards (carte de visite), *were often left behind after a visit, one of the first commercial uses of newly developed photographic methods.* Carte de visite *were collected in large books. Lili'uokalani had seven such books, with pictures collected from the 1850s-1890s. Here are eight from the hundreds in her collection.*

Clockwise from top left: Keoni Ana, John Young's son and Emma's uncle, c. 1850. He served as kuhina nui and Minister of the Interior under Kamehameha III. An unidentified pair. Dignitaries, including this enigmatic pair, were hosted at Washington Place, c. 1870. The high chief of Fiji and his wife, c. 1870.

Clockwise from top left: Queen Emma's cousin, Peter Kaʻeo, developed leprosy and was sent to Kalaupapa but was ultimately released several years before he died. Caesar Kapaʻakea, Liliʻuokalani's birth father, c. 1860; he died in 1866. A unnamed German Duke, c. 1879. The Empress of Austria, c. 1887.

Modernization meant keeping pace with technological advances—of port facilities, plantations, and urban infrastructure. Sugar-generated revenues were needed to pay the cost of loans and government-funded projects. As a first order of business, Kalākaua set off for Washington, D.C. to pursue a treaty of reciprocity with the United States, following through on the demands of planters and the failed initiatives of his predecessors.

The two-cent-per-pound savings the Reciprocity Treaty of 1875 secured made Hawaiian sugar highly profitable, prompting rapid expansion of acreage and output, with plantations incorporating new technologies in the field and in the mill. That, in turn, meant increasing the number of Chinese workers first brought to Hawai'i in the mid-1860s on three-to-five-year contracts. Some sought brides from their homelands while others married into Hawaiian families. By 1879, nearly 10,000 Chinese represented about seventeen percent of the kingdom's resident population. Most were not citizens of the kingdom they now called home.

A demographic time bomb was ticking, for despite inroads in health care, the Native population continued its decline. By 1879, there were 5,000 fewer Hawaiians than when the decade began. Kalākaua had signaled his concern with a program called Ho'oulu Lāhui, Increase the Race, but slogans could not assure success. He and Kapi'olani, Lili'uokalani and Dominis, Pauahi and Bishop, and others remained childless. Joy was widespread when Likelike, wife of Scotsman Archibald Cleghorn, gave birth to Ka'iulani in 1875. The beloved princess would be the only royal child of her generation.

Lili'uokalani admired her niece, spending time with her and writing to her when she was away at school in England, encouraging and gently advising her as she had done with her mother whose marriage had proved even more demoralizing than Liliʻuokalaniʻs. Victorian men didn't like nor respect female competition while aliʻi women felt empowered to express themselves. For both sisters this was an unbridgeable divide. Liliʻuokalaniʻs bond to Kaʻiulani strengthened after Likelike died in 1887 when Kaʻiulani was twelve.

As heir to the throne, Liliʻuokalani traveled around the islands, impressed by the aloha and generosity that welcomed her entourage. The love of the people for their chiefs demanded reciprocation by the chief to her people. A chief whose people suffered was shamed. Liliʻuokalani understood this.

The year 1879 proved to be a prosperous one. Thanks to reciprocity Hawaiian sugar became a path to wealth to the planters and marginally to their foreign-born workers. Little filtered down to the Hawaiian community which provided relatively few workers for the plantations, the Hawaiians not liking company's domination nor the repetitive nature of plantation life.

Liliʻuokalaniʻs childless marriage continued to be problematic. In 1878, she sought comfort in a hānai daughter she named Lydia. The child's father, Luther Aholo, was secretary to Dominis in his role as Governor of Oʻahu and Maui. The infant's mother died soon after giving birth, and Liliʻuokalani moved forward despite opposition from Dominis, Pauahi, and Kalākaua. While Liliʻuokalani had a compassionate love of children, she was not skilled at parenting. As a result, her relationship with Lydia Aholo and the two hānai sons that followed was not always easy.

At forty-one when the next decade began, Liliʻuokalani was ready for the challenges that came with being heir to the throne. Inquisitive by nature, she sought knowledge as a path to wisdom from a variety of eclectic sources, using the Bible's message of compassion and grace as a guiding principle, believing in the integrity of Christian ideals.

A student of four decades of history that had touched her directly, she backed her beliefs with thoughtful analysis. In this, she was extending herself into what was a man's world, and she was considered perhaps too strong-willed and independent in asserting her self. Hawaiian tradition certainly had gender definitions, but mana prevailed, with strong-willed women like Kaʻahumanu as role models for the Princess Royale as the first three years as heir moved her into the 1880s. What was clear to Liliʻuokalani was that only an empowered monarch could defend the interests of her people.

Above: Honolulu Harbor, c. 1875. **Right:** Honolulu's Chinatown, c. 1875. Many plantation workers remained after their labor contracts were fulfilled. **Below:** Infrastructure upgrades and modernization required financing. Charles Reed Bishop opened Hawai'i's first bank in 1858, with new upscale offices opened downtown in the 1870s.

A newspaper report announcing the signing of a treaty of reciprocity between Hawai'i and the U.S.

TREATY OF RECIPROCITY
BETWEEN THE UNITED STATES OF AMERICA AND THE HAWAIIAN KINGDOM.

The United States of America and His Majesty the King of the Hawaiian Islands, equally animated by the desire to strengthen and perpetuate the friendly relations which have heretofore uniformly existed between them, and to consolidate their commercial intercourse, have resolved to enter into a Convention for Commercial Reciprocity. For this purpose, the President of the United States has conferred full powers on Hamilton Fish, Secretary of State, and His Majesty the King of the Hawaiian Islands has conferred like powers on Honorable Elisha H. Allen, Chief Justice of the Supreme Court, Chancellor of the Kingdom, Member of the Privy Council of State, His Majesty's Envoy Extraordinary and Minister Plenipotentiary to the United States of America, and Honorable Henry A. P. Carter, Member of the Privy Council of State, His Majesty's Special Commissioner to the United States of America.

" *A nation-snatching treaty... [he ku 'ikahi ka'ili aupuni], one that will take away the rights of the people causing the throne to be deprived of powers that it has always held as fundamental.*"

—NATIVE ADVISOR JOSEPH NĀWAHĪ, 1875

"*At noon of the tenth day of April, 1877, the booming of the cannon was heard which announced that I was heir apparent to the throne of Hawaii...From this moment dates my official title of Liliuokalani that being the name by which I was formally proclaimed princess and heir apparent to the throne of my ancestors.*"

Lili'uokalani, heir to the throne, c. 1879. A regal look that some in the opposition interpreted as arrogant. Empowered by her ali'i status, she projected the authority of her ancestry.

57

1881: Liliʻuokalani rules as regent in Kalākaua's absence.

CHAPTER SIX
THE 1880s

Evolution of a Future Queen

IN 1880 LILI'UOKALANI WOULD BE FORTY-TWO and she would soon take on more than the title of royalty. For ten months, starting in January 1881, when Kalākaua set off on a trip around the world, she ruled in his stead and was privy to the process of governing for the first time. Almost immediately, she was faced with a health crisis as smallpox appeared and with it the threat of yet another epidemic. She responded with a carefully implemented quarantine that spared the city. As regent, she proved adept and received praise from many quarters.

Curiosity, as well as diplomatic and economic objectives, motivated Kalākaua's travels. The planters needed still more workers, with Kalākaua negotiating agreements with the governments of Japan and Portugal for new sources of plantation workers. As with the Chinese, many would stay on after their contracts were fulfilled, bringing in picture brides and starting families adding to the ethnic mix that was further reducing the percentage of Native Hawaiians in the kingdom. By 1889, the Hawaiians were, for the first time, a minority of Hawai'i's residents, outnumbered by Chinese, Japanese, Portuguese, Americans, and Europeans—most of whom were not citizens.

Kalākaua's political objective was to establish an identity for Hawai'i as an independent kingdom, an equal in the family of nations. He understood the covetous ambitions of imperial nations and presented a strong and favorable impression as he met with princes, kings, maharajas, and politicians in Asia and Europe before heading to Washington, D.C., where he was welcomed by President Chester Arthur. It was an eye-opening introduction to the world and a lesson in the substance and symbols of power.

Kalākaua's return was the start of confrontational government, with an increasingly vocal opposition in the legislature, loosely known as "the missionary party," becoming increasingly disillusioned by the cost of maintaining the monarchy and a monarch whose tastes went beyond his and the government's means.

It was not only the king's fault. Some overruns were inevitable because the kingdom's infrastructure—from deepening harbors to accommodate larger ships, to installing water and sewage lines, to paving gas-lit streets— were all part of the kingdom's modernization.

Technological advances further enhanced American involvement in the sugar economy. Plantation agriculture's expansion demanded new mills, railroads, roads, and new water sources for water-hungry cane. All were big ticket items paid for by loans financed by American banks, further integrating the Hawaiian and American economies. Lili'uokalani understood the danger: In both economic and demographic terms the kingdom was losing control of Hawai'i's destiny.

The king's choice of Walter Murray Gibson as Prime Minister and the influence of sugar magnate Claus Spreckels were also cause for opposition. Gibson was seen as a schemer and fraud who inflated Kalākaua's ambitions. Spreckels controlled a sugar empire, with thousands of acres in Hawai'i, refineries in California, a fleet of ships that linked the two, and free access to the American market. It was largely Spreckels' money that both the government and Kalākaua had borrowed to finance recurring shortfalls.

The opposition resented and distrusted Spreckels' power and his influence over the king, who personally owed Spreckels more than one million dollars. Kalākaua's indebtedness led to more than one scandal, damaging the monarchy's credibility. Lili'uokalani, of a far more serious disposition, viewed her brother's lack of self-restraint and questionable judgment as problematic. But she had little influence with him and remained always respectful of his title, treating him with the emotions of a loving sister.

Financial issues confronted the king soon after his return with 'Iolani Palace—an impressively designed residence that supported Kalākaua's ambitions as king. Construction that begun in 1879, was nearing completion. He had to request additional funding several times as costs spiraled to a budget-busting $340,000. The following year, in the ninth year of his reign, the king sought and received funding for a gala coronation, an event inspired by his travels abroad where he experienced the pomp accorded his fellow

Above: Kalākaua at his coronation ceremony in 1883. His travels abroad, visiting kings and maharajas, opened his eyes to the trappings of monarchy which he sought to emulate. Kapiʻolani had a reserved nature and felt more at home in Hawaiian society. Of aliʻi birth, she was a loving partner, but the marriage was childless. **Right:** Miriam Likelike's daughter, Princess Kaʻiulani, at the age of eleven in 1887, after her mother's death. She was second in line to the throne after Liliʻuokalani and became Liliʻuokalani's heir in 1891.

Above: January, 1881—King Kalākaua set forth on a ten-month trip around the world, negotiating a labor agreement with the government of Japan and mingling with his fellow royals. Liliʻuokalani actively ruled in his absence. **Right:** Walter Murray Gibson, c. 1885, served as Kalākaua's Prime Minister and Foreign Minister, encouraging the king's appetite for living beyond his means. The missionary party, the "downtown boys" as Liliʻuokalani called them, hated Gibson and demanded his dismissal, ultimately driving him from the islands with a physical assault that soon after led to his death in California.

royals. Gold crowns inlaid with precious stones were ordered from Britain, along with a gold scepter and royal ring. There were also the ahu ʻula (feather capes) and kahili that linked the Westernized present to the Hawaiian past.

Liliʻuokalani, as heir to the throne, had a prominent place in the ceremony as did Likelike and Kapiʻolani's royal kin, her hānai nephews, Kūhiō and David Kawānanakoa. Post-coronation events included a grand ball and lūʻau, and the unveiling of the statue of Kamehameha, positioned across the street from the palace fronting Aliʻiōlani Hale. Hula was integrated into the ceremonies—a tradition that provoked scorn from the missionary party as retrograde. While Kamehameha V had begun to integrate Hawaiian elements into court protocol, Kalākaua provided it with prominence.

He and Liliʻuokalani were true caretakers of the Hawaiian past, each working to preserve what they had learned from Pākī, Konia, and others of the last generation directly linked to the ways of old. Kalākaua authored *The Legends and Myths of Hawaii* in 1888. The following year he published a sixty-page version of the *Kumulipo,* the Hawaiʻi chant of creation that identified the ancestry of the chiefly families and was left to him by his grandfather, ʻAikanaka.

Several years later, Liliʻuokalani provided a masterful English translation of its 2,102 lines that was published in 1897. Both befriended and contributed to the writings of Abraham Fornander, an arrival from Sweden who married into the Hawaiian community and became a chronicler of the Hawaiian past.

In 1882, having taken Lydia Aholo as hānai and making members of her family part of her retinue she took Joseph Kaipo ʻAeʻa, son of another retainer in her court, as her second hānai. Something of a rascal, he was Liliʻuokalani's favorite, leaving her bereft when he died in 1914 of Bright's Disease, unmarried and childless.

Taking Kaipo as hānai followed soon after another retainer in her court gave birth to a child fathered by John Dominis. It was not Dominis' only affair, a reality that intimates knew and which no doubt caused Liliʻuokalani considerable anguish, seeking comfort in Christian idealism. Initially she sought to hānai the child, but faced opposition from Dominis, who never

'Iolani Palace (above), an Italianate building, was completed at a cost of over $340,000 in 1882. Well over budget, continued requests for legislative funding drew increasing opposition—not just to Kalākaua, but to the concept of monarchy. Belief in the ideals of a republican America remained strong in the second and third generation of missionary descendants who left Hawai'i to receive college level degrees in the U.S. then returned as lawyers and businessmen with positive perspectives on America's role in Hawai'i's future.

Above and left: In the ninth year of his reign, Kalākaua had a coronation ceremony at his newly-built palace. Lili'uokalani and Likelike participated in the coronation ceremony. Thousands came and enjoyed the festivities that marked the event which was funded by the government. Equally offensive to the opposition was Kalākaua's inclusion of hula, considered obscene by the missionaries, as an integral part of the celebration. Both Kalākaua and Lili'uokalani were knowledgeable about and took pride in their Hawaiian ancestry.

"*My sister, the Princess Likelike, had sent to San Francisco for her wardrobe, which, like mine, consisted of two complete costumes, one of which was ... handsomely trimmed with pearls; her full evening dress was of silk, in a color or shade styled at that time "moonlight-on-the-lake..."*

Both Kalākaua and Liliʻuokalani contributed to Abraham Fornander's (**above left**) writings on Hawaiian history and culture. Fornander was one of several transplants who helped preserve fast-fading knowledge of the ways of old. **right:** A Hawaiian family outside a traditional hale, c. 1885. Rural living was still a self-sustaining enterprise.

"Our past experience with the disease had shown us how fatal it might become to the Hawaiian people, and whatever inconveniences it became necessary at all hazards to prevent its spread. Summoning the cabinet, I had all arrangements perfected to stay the progress of the epidemic."

In the 1870s, Hansen's Disease (leprosy) was brought in on a ship from China. Both Emma and Liliʻuokalani visited the leper colony at Kalawao. Father Damien is pictured with Kalaupapa's residents in 1889 shortly before he died. Soon after taking over as regent in 1881, a smallpox epidemic threatened. On her orders, quarantine and isolation were implemented to stop its spread. Her response proved largely effective.

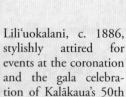

Lili'uokalani, c. 1886, stylishly attired for events at the coronation and the gala celebration of Kalākaua's 50th birthday in 1886.

claimed parenting John 'Aimoku. Ultimately, Lili'uokalani left the boy in the care of his grandmother. While Lili'uokalani provided for him financially, it was not until 1910, eighteen years after John Owen's death in 1892 that Lili'uokalani made John 'Aimoku Dominis her hānai son, legally adding Dominis as his parental surname. He too came to an early end, dying in 1917 six months before Lili'uokalani.

The 1880s was a time of personal loss for Lili'uokalani. First was Ruth Ke'elikōlani who passed in 1883, followed by Bernice Pauahi Bishop who died of cancer in 1884. In 1885, Queen Emma was gone with sister, Miriam Likelike, dying in 1887 at thirty-nine from a wasting disease that she believed was the result of spell placed on her by an enemy. In old Hawai'i, priests called kahuna 'ana'ana were believed to possess such powers. Finally, in 1889, the irascible Mary Dominis made an exit at the age of eighty-six.

In 1886 the king planned a gala to celebrate his fiftieth birthday. Two weeks of festivities ended in a grand lū'au for 1,500 as expenditure soared. Then in 1887, the king created a one-ship navy and sent it on a mission to Samoa to create a Polynesian confederation with himself as king. The embassy was sent packing with Germany and the United States already

"Queen Emma never recovered from her great disappointment that our family had been chosen as the royal line to succeed that of the Kamehamehas."

"I was tenderly attached to my sister [right], so much that her decease had an unfavorable effect on my health."

Death stalked Hawaiian royals and commoners alike. Ruth Keʻelikōlani died in 1883 at fifty-nine (**top left**). Ruth's cousin Bernice succumbed to cancer in 1884 at the age of fifty-two, pictured here with Charles Reed Bishop, c. 1885 (**top right**). Queen Emma died in 1885 at the age of forty-nine (**bottom left**). Miriam Likelike died in 1887, one month after her thirty-sixth birthday (**bottom right**).

Claus Spreckels, c. 1885. By the mid-1880s, Spreckels controlled much of Hawai'i's sugar output with plantations, refineries, and the shipping of sugar between Hawai'i and California. In addition, half of the royal government's debt was due to Spreckels, with the king personally indebted to him for more than one-million dollars. Spreckels' Honolulu home was a cottage compared to his San Francisco mansion.

Acreage planted in sugar greatly expanded in the 1880s, requiring the importation of thousands of workers to Hawai'i. Many remained after their contracts ended, bringing wives to Hawai'i from their homelands and raising families, creating a demographic shift in the kingdom's population. By the end of the decade, Hawaiians represented less than half of the kingdom's population.

in the process of divvying up Samoa. The result was an expensive and embarrassing retreat.

In June of 1887, Lili'uokalani proved herself an impressive ambassador for the kingdom, accompanying Queen Kapi'olani to the United States and London where they were honored guests at Queen Victoria's Golden Jubilee, reaffirming links between Great Britain and Hawai'i that began in 1778 with Captain James Cook's landing. A confident conversationalist with wide-ranging knowledge, she spoke amiably with emperors and kings, taking the pressure off Kapi'olani who was not fluent in English.

Events in Hawai'i, however, demanded a rapid departure after word reached the royal party that the king had been forced, under threat of harm, to sign a new constitution that empowered the legislature and made the monarch little more than a figurehead.

"There were duchesses with shining tiara, marchionesses with coronets of flashing stones, noble ladies with costly necklaces or emerald ear-drops, little women who seemed almost bowed down under lofty circlets of diamonds over their brows…I have never seen such a grand display of valuable gems…"

Above and left: Queen Victoria's Golden Jubilee in 1887 marked her fifty years on the throne. Lili'uokalani accompanied Kapi'olani to England for the gala celebrations, impressing her fellow royals with her mastery of English and her wide-ranging knowledge. She also enjoyed the company of creative types, like Robert Louis Stevenson (**below**).

Liliʻuokalani understood the implications for her people for the Bayonet Constitution, as it came to be called, also disenfranchised many Hawaiians due to restrictive property qualifications that also gave voting rights to non-citizens. The new constitution was not sanctioned by the legislature. Rather it was devised by members of the "missionary party" unilaterally making their action a coup d'état by men seeking annexation of the islands by the United States.

When the royal party reached Hawaiʻi a sense of uncertainty prevailed. There were a number of fault lines along what was an evolving ideological divide—republican America versus monarchical Hawaiʻi, for example. For many annexationists there were links maintained with family in the communities they had departed. Many were sent to New England to study at Yale, Harvard, and other universities. Born and raised in Hawaiʻi, they were an entitled elite that returned to Hawaiʻi to succeed at commerce and pursue annexation. That had not been the objective of the missionaries themselves, for they were admonished to remain free of political entanglements. That is why those who served the monarchy first left the Mission. The missionaries were generally loyal to the monarchy, although to varying degrees they were disdainful of the Hawaiian host culture. Their descendants saw the Hawaiians as a dying race, possibly doomed to extinction if demographic trends continued. For the pro-annexationists, the future lay in union with the United States.

In 1887, a new reciprocity treaty was signed between Hawaiʻi and the United States. This time the United States made agreement conditional upon granting the U.S. the exclusive naval rights to Pearl Harbor. Liliʻuokalani was upset and advised against what she saw as a compromise of Hawaiian sovereignty. A change in U.S. tariff laws in 1890 that paid a bounty to American sugar growers, rather than a tariff on incoming goods, eliminated the duty-free advantage of reciprocity. Despite that failure, the U.S. maintained its naval presence at Pearl Harbor, in fact confirming Liliʻuokalani's fears.

As the decade came to an end, the weary king's health began to fail, placing Liliʻuokalani ever closer to an endangered throne.

≫ — ≪

Her Royal Highness Liliʻuokalani.

Lili'uokalani, c. 1885.

CHAPTER SEVEN

Poetry & Music

"To compose was as natural to me as to breathe; and this gift of nature, never having been suffered to fall into disuse, remains a source of the greatest consolation to this day."

I f there was anything that brought uncompromised pleasure to Lili'uokalani's life it was music. More than melodies were involved. There were also the poetic lyrics—compositions usually in both Hawaiian and English—that spoke of her romantic nature and her belief in God's redeeming justice.

It could be said that musical talent ran in the family. All of her adult siblings—Kalākaua, Leleiōhoku, and Likelike—were musically talented. But they didn't compare to the quality and quantity that was Lili'uokalani's musical and poetic legacy. Over the years she composed more than 200 songs, many of lyric quality that added a multicultural weave to her creativity, proving her mastery of English and Hawaiian and helping create a new genre of Hawaiian music that was at once Western and Hawaiian.

In June 1867, the first printing of *He Mele Lāhui Hawai'i* (Song of the Hawaiian Nation. (See page 74) provided the kingdom with the anthem the king had requested. In 1876, King Kalākaua wrote the words to a new anthem, *Hawai'i Pono'ī*, still sung today. In *He Mele Lāhui Hawai'i*, Lili'uokalani's missionary voice rings loud and clear.

"*In the early years of the reign of Kamehameha V, he brought to my notice the fact that the Hawaiian people had no national air [anthem]. Each nation, he said, but ours had its statement of patriotism and love of country in its own music; but we were using for that purpose on state occasions the time-honored British anthem, God save the Queen... The king ...was liberal in his commendations to me on my success. He admired not only the beauty of music, but spoke enthusiastically of the appropriate words, so well adapted to the air and to the purpose for which they were written.*"

— JUNE 1866

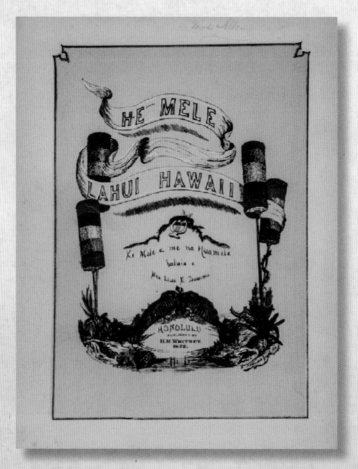

An 1872 copy of *He Mele Lāhui Hawai'i*.

HE MELE
LĀHUI HAWAIʻI

Ka Makua mana loa
Maliu mai iā mākou
E hāliu aku nei
Me ka naʻau haʻahaʻa
E mau ka maluhia
O nei pae ʻāina
Mai Hawaiʻi a Niʻihau
Ma lalo o kou malu

Hui
E mau ke ea o ka ʻāina
Ma kou pono mau
A ma kou mana nui
E ola e ola ka mōʻī

E ka haku mālama mai
I ko mākou nei mōʻī
E mau kona noho ʻana
Maluna o ka noho aliʻi
Hāʻawi mai i ke aloha
Maloko a kona naʻau
A ma kou ahonui
E ola e ola ka mōʻī
Hoʻoho e mau ke

Ma lalo o kou aloha nui
Na Liʻi o ke Aupuni
Me nā makaʻāinana
Ka lehulehu nō a pau
Kiaʻi mai iā lākou
Me ke aloha ahonui
E ola nō mākou
I kou mana mau
E mau ke ea

SONG OF
THE HAWAIIAN NATION

Almighty Father bend thine ear
And listen to a nation's prayer
That lowly bows before thy throne
And seeks thy fostering care
Grant your peace throughout the land
Over these sunny sea girt isles
Keep the nation's life, oh Lord,
And on our sovereign smile

Chorus
Grant your peace throughout the land
Over these sunny isles
Keep the nation's life, oh Lord
And upon our sovereign smile

Guard him with your tender care
Give him length of years to reign
On the throne his fathers won
Bless the nation once again
Give the king your loving grace
And with wisdom from on high
Prosperous lead his people on
As beneath your watchful eye
Grant your peace throughout the land

Bless O Lord our country's chiefs
Grant them wisdom so to live
That our people may be saved
And to You the glory give
Watch over us day by day
King and people with your love
For our hope is all in You
Bless us, You who reign above
Grant your peace throughout the land

Music provided Liliʻuokalani with access to an expression of romantic sentiments that her marriage, and Victorian life in general denied most woman. The most famous of her songs, *Aloha ʻOe,* written in 1878, uses a poignant melody to idealize a moment of farewell written when Liliʻuokalani was the thirty-eight-year-old heir to the throne. The imagery and lyric style are very much Hawaiian with the Queen adding two lines in English—a stylistic device she popularized, adding to the hybrid nature of the song.

ALOHA ʻOE	*UNTIL WE MEET AGAIN*
Haʻaheo e ka ua i nā pali	Proudly swept the rain by the cliffs
Ke nihi aʻela i ka nahele	As it glided through the trees
E hahai (uhai) ana paha i ka liko	Still following ever the bud
Pua ʻāhihi lehua o uka	The ʻāhihi lehua of the vale
Hui	**Chorus**
Aloha ʻoe, aloha ʻoe	Farewell to you, farewell to you
E ke onaona noho i ka lipo	The charming one who dwells in the shaded bowers
One fond embrace,	One fond embrace,
A hoʻi aʻe au	ʻEre I depart
Until we meet again	Until we meet again
ʻO ka haliʻa aloha i hiki mai	Sweet memories come back to me
Ke hone aʻe nei i kuʻu manawa	Bringing fresh remembrances of the past
ʻO ʻoe nō kuʻu ipo aloha	Dearest one, yes, you are mine own
A loko e hana nei	From you, true love shall never depart
Maopopo kuʻu ʻike i ka nani	I have seen and watched your loveliness
Nā pua rose o Maunawili	The sweet rose of Maunawili
I laila hiaʻai nā manu	And ʻtis there the birds of love dwell
Mikiʻala i ka nani o ka liko	And sip the honey from your lips

Left: Liliʻuokalani's hand-written English translation of the first verses of *Aloha ʻOe*, 1878. Below: A printed copy of *Aloha ʻOe* from 1887. *Aloha ʻOe* is Liliʻuokalani's, and perhaps Hawaiʻi's, most famous song. Many dozens of musical transcriptions have been printed over the years.

c. 1900

c. 1905

c. 1912

c. 1915

c. 1910

c. 1910

c. 1916

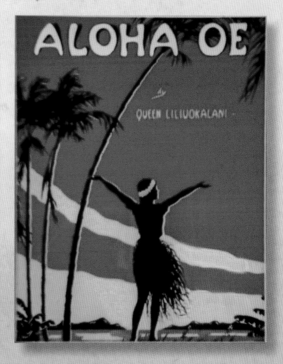

c. 1920

KE ALOHA O KA HAKU

'O kou aloha nō
Aia i ka lani
A 'o Kou 'oia 'i'o
He hemolelo ho'i

Ko'u noho mihi 'ana
A pa'ahao 'ia
'O 'oe ku'u lama
Kou nani ko'u ko'o

Mai nānā 'ino'ino
Nā hewa o kānaka
Akā e huikala
A ma'ema'e nō

No laila e ka Haku
Ma lalo o kou 'ēheu
Kō mākou maluhia
A mau loa aku nō
'Āmene

THE QUEEN'S PRAYER

Your loving mercy
Is as high as Heaven
And your truth
So perfect

I live in sorrow
Imprisoned
You are my light
Your glory, my support

Behold not with malevolence
The sins of man
But forgive
And cleanse

And so, o Lord
Protect us beneath your wings
And let peace be our portion
Now and forever more
Amen

MUʻOLAULANI	MUʻOLAULANI
He mea nui ke aloha	This great love of yours
Ke hiki mai i oʻu nei	Has come here to me
Meheʻo kuʻu lei kaimana ala	It is like my diamond necklace
Kāhiko o kuʻu kino	To adorn my person
Kuʻu lei popohe i ka laʻi	My lei so shapely in the calm
Nohea i Muʻolaulani	Handsome at Muʻolaulani
Ka beauty lā he mau ia	It is a beauty, always a thing forever
No nā kau ā kau	For all seasons

Above: Two of the Queen's more than 200 compositions. One tells of the impact of flowers brought to her in prison from her Waikīkī home, Paoakalani. In the other, Hawaiian imagery tells a story of her Kapālama home, Muʻolaulani, written ten years earlier. Ironically, it was the weapons found buried on the grounds at Muʻolaulani that would help convict her at trial in 1895. *Farewell to Thee* transported to the U.S. Mainland, c. 1905. The total of twelve performances reveals the popularity of the exotic Hawaiian theme once Hawaiʻi became a territory of the U.S.

Opposite page: *The Queen's Prayer,* written in 1895 while she was imprisoned in ʻIolani Palace.

AN ACCOUNT
OF
THE CREATION OF THE WORLD
ACCORDING TO
HAWAIIAN TRADITION
TRANSLATED FROM ORIGINAL MANUSCRIPTS PRESERVED
EXCLUSIVELY IN HER MAJESTY'S FAMILY
BY
LILIUOKALANI OF HAWAII

PRAYER OF DEDICATION

THE CREATION
FOR
KA I: MAMAO
FROM HIM TO HIS DAUGHTER
ALAPAI WAHINE
LILIUOKALANI'S GREAT-GRANDMOTHER
COMPOSED BY
KEAULUMOKU IN 1700 AND TRANSLATED BY LILIUOKALANI DURING
HER IMPRISONMENT IN 1895 AT IOLANI PALACE AND AFTERWARDS
AT WASHINGTON PLACE HONOLULU   WAS COMPLETED
AT WASHINGTON D.C. MAY 20 1897

KUMULIPO

Lili'uokalani's exacting translation into English of the 2,102 lines of the *Kumulipo*, accomplished while she was imprisoned at 'Iolani Palace, was published in June 1897. Lili'uokalani, at age sixty-two the longest-lived of all her royal peers spent the years after her release unsuccessfully seeking political and financial restitution. Always spiritually linked to the Hawaiian past, she transcribed the telling of the *Kumulipo*, the Hawaiian chant of creation. The *Kumulipo* has many interesting parallels to the *Old Testament*, so thoroughly taught by her childhood tutors, yet with a Darwinian twist. Her telling provided a glimpse into the sophistication of Hawaiian belief that paved the way to Christianity.

First Verse, First Era

At the time that turned the heat of the earth,
At the time when the heavens turned and changed,
At the time when the light of the sun was subdued
To cause light to break forth,
At the time of the night of Makalii (winter)
Then began the slime which established the earth,
The source of deepest darkness.
Of the depth of darkness, of the depth of darkness,
Of the darkness of the sun, in the depth of night,
    It is night,
    So was night born.

First Verse, Eighth Era

The child of Uli, of Uli of Ke,
The child in the time of numerous night,
The child in the time of riding distant surf in the night.
Beings were born to increase.
Male was born of Waiololi,
Female was born of Waiolola,

Then was born the night of gods,
Men that stood,
Of men lying down,
They slept long sleep in the distant time,
And went staggering when they walked.
The forehead of the gods is red.
That of man is dark.
Their chins are light.
Then calmness spread in the time of Kapokinikini—
Calm in the time of Kapoheenalu mamao,
And it was called there Lailai.
Lailai was born a woman,
Kii was born a man.
Kane a god was born.
Kanaloa was born a god, the great Kaheehaunawela (Octopus). 'Tis day.

Final Verse, 16th Era

Kawaukaohele was born, also Keleanuinohoanaapiapi,—
The woman that lived at Kalamakua,
From whence Laielohelohe was born and who married
Piilani. Piikea was born and married Umi; to
Kumalaenuia Umi, who owned those precipices from whence slaves were held.
Kumalaenui of Umi was the husband of Kunuunuipuawalau.
Their son, Makua, was the only high chief (wohi kukahi) of the island.
Kapohelemai,
Whose power and right to execute,
And lord of the famed lands of Pakini,
Of the sliding Ohia and the weaving of the islands of Hawaii
To Ahu to Ahu of I, of Lono, Of Lonoikamakahiki.

A regal presence
as the 1890s begin.

CHAPTER EIGHT
1890–1893

A Tragically Short Reign

"What have I done that was so wrong,
that I should lose my country for our people."

O N JANUARY 20, 1891, IN THE SEVENTEENTH YEAR OF HIS REIGN, Kalākaua died in his Palace Hotel room in San Francisco. The years of combative government took their toll, aging the fifty-five-year-old king beyond his years. The once unexpected came to pass and Lili'uokalani took her oath as Queen of Hawai'i.

No one in Hawai'i was informed of his passing, the sad news revealed when the USS *Charleston*, carrying his body, was spotted flying black flags. The gala welcome that had been planned instead became a funeral procession with Lili'uokalani accompanying the body from the port to the palace.

With fears of a coup, the royalists insisted Lili'uokalani take the throne immediately. Initially she resisted, wanting to postpone the event out of respect for Kalākaua's passing and the personal grief that it had brought, but it was considered politically necessary to make the transition as quickly as possible. So on January 29, 1891, Lili'uokalani took the oath that made her queen according to the terms of the 1887 constitution.

Kalākaua's difficulties quickly flowed into Lili'uokalani's reign, ill will compounded by a personality some considered imperious and too assertive. More immediate was the economic turmoil and the resulting depression in the United States which, in conjunction with the end of the benefits accorded Hawaiian sugar by the McKinley tariffs of 1890, severely impacted the Hawaiian economy. For an increasingly vocal opposition, that was yet another reason that Hawai'i should seek annexation by the United States.

Had Lili'uokalani been willing to play a passive role—approving legislative measures and serving as an exotic figurehead—the kingdom might

Left: Kapiʻolani was now Queen Dowager. She continued to live at ʻIolani Palace until forced out by the overthrow. She died in 1899. **Below:** John Owen Dominis. He was already ailing when Liliʻuokalani was proclaimed queen and died eight months into her reign. The loss was both political and personal, for he would have served as a politically knowledgeable and well-connected advisor.

"Three days before his departure the king came to see me, and told me of his intention to visit the United States. I did all I could to dissuade him from the journey. I reminded him of his failing health, and informed him that I was not in my usual vigor…"

Above: Kalākaua, aging poorly, set out for San Francisco in November of 1890 seeking a remedy for his ill-health. Liliʻuokalani begged him not to go, fearing he would not return alive. **Right:** At the start of her reign, seeking to assure continuity to the dynasty, Liliʻuokalani named her niece, Princess Kaʻiulani, the only royal child of her generation, as heir to the throne. Kaʻiulani had matured into a beautiful, creative and well-educated young woman, a perfect heir to the throne.

A meeting was called with Liliʻuokalani and Dominis present.

"What is the object of this meeting?" she asked. "He said that they had come together to witness my taking of the oath of office. I told him at once that I did not wish to take the oath just then, and asked why such proceedings could not be deferred until after my brother's funeral. He said that others had decided that I must take my official oath then and there."

January 29, 1893. Liliʻuokalani, by the Grace of God, Hawaiʻi's eighth monarch and first ruling queen.

"I was compelled to take the oath to the constitution, the adoption of which had led to my brother's death…I was so overcome by the death on my dear brother, so dazed with the suddenness of the news which had come upon us in a moment, that I hardly realized what was going on about me, nor did I at all appreciate for the moment my situation."

Charles Gulick was one of the few missionary descendants supportive of the throne. Those Lili‘uokalani came to rely on were her peers, a mix of Hawaiian and non-Native supporters. The four most prominent were: (**clockwise from top left**) Samuel Parker, three-quarters Hawaiian and a Big Island rancher who served as Foreign Minister and Minister of Finance; Hermann Widemann, German-born, who served on the Supreme Court and the Bureaus of Health and Immigration; John Adams Cummins, a wealthy Hawaiian businessman who personally hosted Lili‘uokalani on several occasions, was in the legislature, and served in several cabinet posts; and John Mott-Smith, out of New York, who became Hawai‘i's first practicing dentist—a skill self-taught, supplemented by serving as the Kingdom's roving diplomat.

"At all these places the people who came to receive us were delighted to have the opportunity to show their loyalty and manifest their love."

The Queen and Suite at Naalehu

A royal visit to Nā'alehu on the island of Hawai'i. Soon after becoming queen, Lili'uokalani toured her island kingdom, reaffirming the traditional bond between the people and their chiefs.

The Royal Household Guard at the barracks adjacent to the palace. The royal military had been a casualty of the Bayonet Constitution coup.

Royal Hawaiian Band.

The Royal Hawaiian Band continued under Bandmaster Henry Berger. He and the Queen had a close personal friendship.

have survived. But Lili'uokalani, as ali'i nui and as mo'i wahine (high chief and queen), considered protecting her people a sacred responsibility and she chafed under the restraints of the Bayonet Constitution looking for ways to legally assert the throne's power and thereby the interests of the Hawaiian people. This was bad enough emanating from Kalākaua, but coming from a woman at a time when politics and diplomacy were purely a man's game only compounded the revolutionary fervor of the opposition.

The leader of the opposition was Lorrin Thurston, grandson of Asa Thurston who arrived in Hawai'i in 1820 with the First Company of American missionaries sent to convert and civilize the "pagan" Hawaiians. Lorrin Thurston was a Columbia University-trained lawyer who was influential in imposing the Bayonet Constitution. Now he went one step further and took aim at overthrowing the monarchy and seeking annexation by the United States. Thurston's disdain for Kalākaua was immediately transferred to Lili'uokalani whose determination to rule as well as to reign only confirmed his opposition, which coalesced around an executive group called the Committee of Safety. In 1887 they had organized the Hawaiian League as an organization arm of the annexationists. More significantly, they were backed by a well-armed militia of more than one thousand called the Honolulu Rifles. Initially formed to support the monarchy, it had morphed into an annexationist militia with more manpower and firepower than the Royal Household Guard that protected the Queen.

From the start of her reign Lili'uokalani faced paralyzing opposition, with the legislature voting out one Cabinet after another seeking to weed out her supporters. This ongoing delegitimization of her efforts was a tactic that left the kingdom without a functioning government. It was demoralizing for the queen and her supporters, the impasse playing into the hands of the annexationists and leaving the queen with fewer and fewer committed allies.

The problem was compounded in August, 1891, when John Dominis passed away. Whatever his emotional shortcomings toward Lili'uokalani, he was politically astute and provided a political perspective that was now missing. His passing left her increasingly isolated despite the support of a loyal cadre of friends and supporters.

Although she took her oath of office as defined by the Constitution of 1887 she rightly considered it illegitimate, imposed without legislative

Right: A baker's dozen: The thirteen members of the Committee of Safety (also called the Committee of Thirteen), the executive leadership of the Annexationist Club formed in 1892, was backed by the para-military Honolulu Rifles.

The mastermind was Lorrin Thurston (above left), missionary-grandson born in Hawai'i, who, for ideological and financial reasons, sought annexation. A member of the missionary party in the legislature, he and P.C. Jones crafted the Bayonet Constitution without legislative approval. It was Thurston who plotted with American Minister and Plenipotentiary, John L. Stevens (above right), to secure American support and recognition of the revolutionaries. Stevens saw manifest destiny casting a wide net, including Hawai'i, making him the perfect ally. Thurston headed to Washington soon after the coup to muster support for annexation. Sanford Dole (above center) served as the respected frontman for the Provisional Government and later as president of the Republic of Hawai'i.

"The Hawaiian pear is now fully ripe, and this is the golden hour for the United States."

—JOHN STEVENS

"But of Minister John L. Stevens it must be said that he was either mentally incapable of recognizing what is to be expected of a gentleman, to say nothing of a diplomat, or he was decidedly in league with those persons who had conspired against the peace of Hawaii..."

—LILI'UOKALANI **91**

approval and outside the framework of the Constitution of 1864 which was then the law of the land. From an historical perspective, she saw precedents back to 1840 with each previous constitution unilaterally promulgated and implemented by her royal predecessors.

Events came to a head in December, 1892, weeks short of the second anniversary of her reign. After a dispiriting dismissal of yet another Cabinet, the Queen decided the time had come to promulgate a new constitution. She produced a balanced document that clearly identified an understanding of constitutional government, provided a meaningful balance of power between crown and legislature, and provided for the re-enfranchisement of the Hawaiians—the monarchy's primary constituents.

Advised against taking a precipitous action, she quickly found herself without any meaningful political support. Even her closest advisors considered her effort at constitutional change unrealistic. Finding herself without the support of her Cabinet, with the legislative opposition loudly calling for an end to the monarchy, she was forced to retreat. On January 13, 1893, she withdrew her constitution and agreed to work within the framework of the Bayonet Constitution.

Events moved quickly beyond her concession and control. An effort to place Ka'iulani on the throne, initially floated by Sanford Dole, was quickly rejected. Sensing victory, the annexationists were not looking for a compromise. Thurston was an adept and lucky strategist pursuing his political objectives with missionary focus and zeal. His fiery oration at a meeting the night of January 16, 1893, insulted the queen personally and called for revolutionary change.

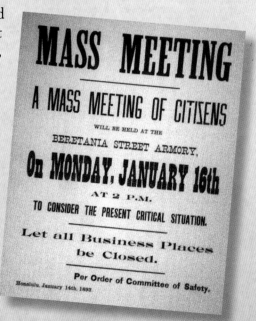

MASS MEETING

A MASS MEETING OF CITIZENS

WILL BE HELD AT THE

BERETANIA STREET ARMORY,

On **MONDAY, JANUARY 16th**

AT 2 P.M.

TO CONSIDER THE PRESENT CRITICAL SITUATION.

Let all Business Places be Closed.

Per Order of Committee of Safety.

Honolulu, January 14th, 1893.

At a mass rally, Thurston fired the crowd to violence, knowing he would have the support of U.S. Marines.

"*In the year 1893, on the 15th of January, at the request of a large majority of the Hawaiian people, and by and with the consent of my cabinet, I proposed to make certain changes in the constitution of the Hawaiian kingdom, which were suggested to me as being for the advantage and benefit of the kingdom, and subjects and residents thereof. These proposed changes did not deprive foreigners of any rights or privileges enjoyed by them under the constitution of 1887.*"

"*It is alleged that my proposed constitution was to make such changes as to give the sovereign more power, and to the cabinet or legislature less, and that only subjects, in distinction from temporary residents, could exercise suffrage. In other words, that I was to restore some of the ancient rights of my people…But supposing I had thought it wise to limit the exercise of suffrage to those who owed allegiance to no other country; is that different from the usage in all other civilized nations on earth?… The right to grant a constitution to the nation has been, since the very first one was granted, a prerogative of the Hawaiian sovereigns.*"

"*It may be true that they really believed us unfit to be trusted to administer the grown wealth of the Islands in a safe and proper way. But if we manifested any incompetency, it was not foreseeing that they would be bound by no obligations, by honor, or by oath of allegiance, should an opportunity arise for seizing our country, and bringing it under the authority of the United States.*"

"*If we did not by force resist their final outrage, it was because we could not do so without striking at the military force of the United States.*"

Above, top: The Honolulu Rifles, originally organized in support of the monarchy, had morphed into an armed militia committed to its overthrow. The Rifles outnumbered the Queen's meager military resources. bottom: U.S. Marines were landed to supposedly protect Americans and their property, but were positioned so as to stop a response to the coup. It was Stevens' disgraceful betrayal of a friendly government to which he'd been dispatched that paved the way to annexation.

Behind the scenes he orchestrated a coup, made successful by the support of American troops landed by order of Minister Plenipotentiary of the United States to Hawai'i, John L. Stevens. Stevens advised Thurston of specific objectives that would allow him to declare the revolutionaries the de facto government of the Hawaiian Islands.

Claiming American lives were at risk because of the royal government's actions, Thurston secured Stevens' support for the coup. U.S. Marines were positioned near enough to the palace to be seen by the Queen who was sequestered inside. With only a small, poorly-armed Household Guard to defend her, and wishing to avoid bloodshed, she made what she hoped was only a temporary surrender of authority as Queen.

On January 24, 1893, under protest and pressured by extenuating circumstances, she signed the document of abdication demanded by the newly formed Provisional Government, with missionary son Sanford Dole at the helm and Lorrin Thurston an active influence.

"For myself, I would have chosen death rather than to have signed it; but it was represented to me that by my signing this paper all the persons who had been arrested, all my people now in trouble by reason of their love and loyalty towards me, would be immediately released. Think of my position, — sick, a lone woman in prison, scarcely knowing who was my friend, or who listened to my words only to betray me, without legal advice or friendly counsel, and the stream of blood ready to flow unless it was stayed by my pen."

She had seen the restoration of Kamehameha III by the British government after Paulet's seizure of power in 1843, and had faith in a similar outcome. That hope had a personal component, for Lili'uokalani had met President Grover Cleveland in 1887 and felt, correctly, that he would offer a sympathetic ear to the just cause of Hawai'i's independence.

She would be steadfast in her pursuit of justice in the years that followed her tragically short reign, undeterred even as the world's nations followed the American lead and recognized the Provisional Government formed to replace the monarchy on January 17th. There was little room in the halls of power willing to recognize the rights of an independent queen in a world rapidly being colonized.

Left: January 17, 1893: Four members of the quickly formed Provisional Government, from the left: Minister of the Interior James A. King (1832-1899) originally from Scotland, Foreign Minister Sanford Dole (1844-1926), missionary son and lawyer, W.O. Smith (1848-1929) missionary descendant and lawyer, and P.C. Jones (1837-1922), a missionary son who was a lawyer, businessman, and banker. Dole had served on Hawai'i's Supreme Court. Jones, who had served as Lili'uokalani's Minister of Finance, was a Boston-born businessman and banker. Despite his role in the coup, Lili'uokalani had Smith, who crafted Pauahi's trust, create the Queen Lili'uokalani Trust in 1909. Thurston served as the PG's spokesman in Washington.

Right: January 19, 1893. The Royal Household Guard is disarmed by order of the Provisional Government.

Below: Washington Place, 1893. The remaining sixteen members of the Royal Household Guard were stationed at Washington Place following the overthrow.

"*I, Liliuokalani of Hawaii, by the grace of God and under the constitution of the Hawaiian kingdom Queen, do hereby solemnly protest against any and all acts done against myself and the constitutional government of the Hawaiian kingdom by certain powers claiming to have established a Provisional Government of and for this kingdom.*

That I yield to the superior force of the United States of America, whose Minister Plenipotentiary, His Excellency John L. Stevens, has caused United States troops to be landed at Honolulu, and declared that he would support the said Provisional Government.

Now, to avoid any collision of armed forces, and perhaps the loss of life, I do, under protest and impelled by said forces, yield my authority until such time as the Government of the United States shall, upon the facts being presented to it, undo the action of its representative, and reinstate me in the authority which I claim as the constitutional sovereign of the Hawaiian Islands."

The Provisional Government was quick to take over all functions of government. By May, 1892, it had over-stamped monarchy era postage, giving it a new identity.

Still the Queen to her people, she would prove herself worthy of their admiration, love, and respect in the aftermath of the overthrow.

CHAPTER NINE
JANUARY 18, 1893–1908

A Queen Without a Throne

"It was the intention of the officers of the government to humiliate me by imprisoning me, but my spirit rose above that. I was a martyr to the cause of my people…I have pursued the path of peace and diplomatic discussion, and not that of internal strife."

SURRENDERING THE THRONE TO AVOID VIOLENCE was both a spiritual and practical decision, for Lili'uokalani found herself without political allies and incapable of mounting a meaningful defense. Her surrender came with protest and an effort that sought the intervention of President Grover Cleveland, who was supportive of the monarchy and Hawaiian independence. He considered the revolution's success due in part to the landing of American troops in such a way as to discourage a royal response, and rejected Stevens' actions

The Queen watched from 'Iolani Palace as American Marines set up barricades while revolutionary forces occupied key government buildings. The choice was not arbitrary. Behind the scenes, even before the coup, Lorrin Thurston, representing the Committee of Safety, was in Washington treasonously negotiating annexation with the out-going administration of President Benjamin Harrison. Negotiations continued after the coup, but anti-imperialist Grover Cleveland's inauguration in March of 1893 resulted in the proposed treaty of annexation being withdrawn.

Seeking an appraisal of the situation following Lili'uokalani's protest and appeal, Cleveland sent Georgia's ex-Representative James H. Blount to Hawai'i. Blount held private interviews with all parties. The Blount Report was issued on July 17, 1893, criticizing the coup and the unjustified American military intervention against the lawful and peaceful royal government. The revolutionaries' claims were deemed false at worst, exaggerated at best, Blount adding that the Hawaiians were overwhelming opposed to the overthrow.

Far left: President Grover Cleveland. His support did not result in Liliʻuokalani's restoration. His envoy to Hawaiʻi, James Blount (left) delivered the Blount Report to Cleveland on July 17, 1893. It stated that the revolution was against a lawful and peaceful government and that the use of U.S. Marines was in no way justified or politically acceptable, since it secured the success of the revolutionaries.

In December, seeking to gain Congressional support for American intervention on Liliʻuokalani's behalf, Minister Plenipotentiary Albert Willis delivered Cleveland's request that Liliʻuokalani agree to a general amnesty for all those involved in the coup. She replied that this was not within her constitutional jurisdiction, but that of her cabinet, and that

"...our laws read that those guilty of treason should suffer the penalty of death... He [Willis] then wished to know if I would carry out that law. I said that I would be more inclined personally to punish them by banishment, and confiscation of their property to the government."

July 4, 1894. The Republic of Hawaiʻi is declared.

On Dec. 18, Cleveland, personally dismayed by Stevens' conspiratorial actions, had Willis deliver a letter to Sanford Dole, Foreign Minister of the quickly organized Provisional Government (PG), with Cleveland calling for the PG to restore the Queen. On December 23rd, Dole replied angrily, justifying the overthrow and writing Cleveland, "...that the Provisional Government of the Hawaiian Islands respectfully and unhesitatingly declines to entertain the proposition of the President of the United States that it should surrender its authority to the ex-Queen."

Cleveland, without political leverage, sent the issue to Congress. Not comfortable with the Blount Report's conclusions, in part because they contradicted annexationist sentiment, a Senatorial investigative committee headed by Alabama Senator John Morgan, no friend of darker races, visited Hawai'i late in 1893. The result was the Morgan Report, issued in February of 1894. It drew different conclusions, justifying the revolution as an internal event with the use of troops necessary to protect American property and lives. The outcome was a Congressional resolution, passed in May, ending intervention into the affairs of the PG. It also opposed immediate consideration of annexation. The Morgan Report further undermined sympathy for Lili'uokalani who was lampooned in political publications with the racial arrogance that was the language of imperial times.

With annexation on hold, the leaders of the PG created a new government that would move Hawai'i beyond the provisional stage. On July 4, 1894, the PG was replaced by the Republic of Hawai'i with Sanford Dole sworn in as President. 'Iolani Palace was largely stripped of its furnishings, which were sold and dispersed as so much excess government property. All vestiges of the past were considered a threat. In Washington, Thurston and others continued to lobby for annexation, anticipating a change in American policy provoked by the speciously launched Spanish-American War, which was the result of increasingly expansionist sentiment in the U.S. With the North American continent spanned, many now looked overseas for territorial expansion.

At the start of 1895, Lili'uokalani found herself under legal assault, accused by the government of misprision of treason, defined as having failed to report and/or concealing knowledge of treasonous activities—charges the Queen vigorously denied. On January 16, 1895, one day short of the second anniversary of her overthrow, a carriage carrying Lili'uokalani pulled up to the palace. Dressed in black she was escorted to what had been her throne room, now a courtroom, where she stood trial.

"The feelings of one who has been imprisoned, politically or otherwise, can only be understood by a person who has passed through the ordeal."

Left: January 16, 1895: A carriage delivers Lili'uokalani to 'Iolani Palace. In what had been her throne room, she was put on trial by the Republic of Hawai'i (below) and charged with misprision of treason (accused of knowing and concealing treasonous activities) as reported in a San Francisco newspaper, along with her emphatic denial. The charge was based on a cache of weapons found buried on the grounds of her home in Kapālama.

"It was the intention of the officers of the government to humiliate me by imprisoning me, but my spirit rose above that. I was a martyr to the cause of my people, and was proud of it."

PAUL NEUMANN MAKING HIS ADDRESS ON BEHALF OF THE EX-QUEEN AT HER TRIAL IN THE PALACE.

REGAL FOR AN HOUR AGAIN.

Left: Lili'uokalani was defended by Paul Neumann, a German Jewish lawyer. Initially sent to Hawai'i by Claus Spreckels, he became a loyal supporter of the monarchy, becoming a member of the House of Nobles and serving as Attorney General under both Kalākaua and Lili'uokalani. He also took on diplomatic roles, serving as an emissary for the kingdom overseas which included a trip to Washington soon after the overthrow to plead the Queen's cause. Lili'uokalani denied the charges and identified the illegality of the proceedings and of the government that initiated them. Her denials and lack of proof resulted in a sentence of five years hard labor and a $5,000 fine. The sentence was commuted, as were death and prison sentences meted out to the insurrectionists, when she signed a formal abdication on January 25, 1893.

The root of the charges lay in an insurrection that sought to restore the monarchy led by the quixotic Robert Wilcox. A part-Hawaiian from Maui, Wilcox had spent nearly ten years in Italy at government expense studying military science. Forced to return to Hawai'i in 1887 when the legislature cut funds for his support, he led an abortive uprising in 1889 seeking to rescind the Bayonet Constitution and restore monarchical power. Under-manned and ill-planned, the effort failed to secure Kalākaua's support and quickly failed.

In January, 1895, he organized a similarly small and poorly organized effort to restore Lili'uokalani. That three-day rebellion also failed at the cost of several lives. The Queen considered Wilcox unpredictable and unreliable and would never have countenanced a counter-revolution under his command. After the insurgents were in custody, however, a cache of arms was found buried in the garden of Lili'uokalani's Kapālama residence. Without conclusive evidence, and despite clearly stated denials, she was found guilty, sentenced to five years of hard labor and fined $5,000.

On January 24, she was compelled to sign official abdication papers in a plea bargain deal that resulted in her sentence and the death sentences against Wilcox and others to be commuted. Prince Kūhiō spent one year in prison for his role in the counter-revolution, with Lili'uokalani imprisoned in a two-room suite on the second floor of 'Iolani Palace.

For eight months, Lili'uokalani suffered the injustice and carefully monitored isolation of her palace prison allowed the company of a single lady-in-waiting, with almost no contact with the outside world. A sentry paraded 24/7 outside her floor-to-ceiling windows. It was a reflective time of spiritual renewal as well as creative accomplishments, the heavy weight of the silently passing hours put into quilting, music, poetry, and a masterful translation of the *Kumulipo*, proving Lili'uokalani's poetic understanding of both Hawaiian and English.

Returning to Washington Place in October after nearly nine months of incarceration, she renewed efforts at rectifying the overthrow. By 1895, however, the overthrow was largely accepted as a *fait accompli*, proven by the rapid acceptance of the PG by foreign governments—indicative of pragmatic politics and the prejudicial feelings of the Euro-American nations toward the independence of any Native people.

The insurrection was led by Robert Wilcox (**top left**) from Maui. Starting in the late 1870s, he spent nearly ten years in Italy at government expense studying military science. Forced to return to Hawaiʻi in 1887 when the legislature cut funds for his support, he led an uprising in 1889 seeking to rescind the Bayonet Constitution and restore monarchical power. Under-manned and ill-planned, the effort failed. The pattern was repeated in 1895, with his forces routed and Wilcox surrendering several days later. Prince Kūhiō (**top right**), nephew to Kapiʻolani and hānai to Kalākaua, would be convicted to a year in prison for his support of the insurgency. **Above:** January 7, 1895. Government forces and militiamen atop ʻIolani Palace as the hunt for the insurgents headed toward Diamond Head.

The quilt, now on display at 'Iolani Palace, was begun while Lili'uokalani was imprisoned and completed soon after. Starting with the present and looking back at significant events in Lili'uokalani's life, the beautifully crafted quilt makes a powerful political statement. **Below:** Lili'uokalani at Washington Place, c. 1897, the same year anti-annexationist petitions, signed by tens of thousands, were submitted to the U.S. Congress.

Demographics underlay the fate of the monarchy. Had Lili'uokalani ruled a nation of as many as the 250,000 estimated by Cook in 1778, it might have been a very different story. But at the time of the overthrow fewer than 35,000 Hawaiians, with an additional 6,500 part-Hawaiians were left—far fewer than half of the Kingdom's population which now included tens of thousands of Chinese, Japanese, and Portuguese. No effort was made to deport those who stayed beyond their work contracts. Most were not citizens and were without any historic loyalty to the monarchy. The opposite was true of the Hawaiians, whose loyalty was almost universal, as Lili'uokalani frequently mentioned in her memoir.

Not even the presentation of two petitions to Congress in 1897 and 1898, one with more than 21,000 signatures and a second with more than 17,000 sponsored by the grassroots Hui Aloha 'Āina by its men's and women's divisions, could reverse the momentum of events driven by the American victory against Spain in the Spanish-American War (1898) that transferred Cuba, Puerto Rico, Guam, and the Philippines to American control. Hawai'i was an important stepping stone between North America and the Philippines. The voice of the kingdom's Hawaiians, largely disenfranchised and marginalized by the Republic's decidedly undemocratic constitution, was not heard.

[Previous Page] -- [View PDF] -- [Next Page]

Men
APANA O HONOLULU (District of Honolulu)
MOKUPUNI O OAHU (Island of Oahu)
Sept. 11th 1897
Enoch Johnson, Secretary -- James Keauiluna Kaulia, President

Members of the Hui Aloha ʻĀina, men's division, which secured and submitted more than 500 pages of signatures against annexation. Along with the petition submitted by the women's division, the petitions represented a convincing majority of Hawaiʻi's native population whose support for the Queen was nearly universal.

Opposite page, below: The Queen remained in Washington, D.C. into the summer of 1897, registering an official complaint, as Hawaiʻi's Queen, with the Secretary of State. While courteously received, the momentum of events was quickly moving toward annexation. Liliʻuokalani was back in Hawaiʻi when word was received that by an act of the U.S. Congress, Hawaiʻi had been annexed as a territory of the United States. Liliʻuokalani was at home at Washington Place, surrounded by supporters, while the annexation ceremony was being held at ʻIolani Palace.

Above: Sanford Dole is sworn in as the first governor of the Territory of Hawai'i on the steps of 'Iolani Palace, soon to become the Territorial government's Executive Building. Annexation was celebrated in a musical tribute (right). Some sang of a glorious future, but not everyone felt like singing about the change of political reality. It was two years later that the final annexation process was completed.

Late in 1897, Liliʻuokalani headed to the East Coast to visit Dominis' relatives, before heading to Washington in a final plea for justice as a vote for annexation was making its way through the U.S. Congress. She responded forcefully in a letter clearly stating the injustices committed with American collusion against her and the Hawaiian people. But strong words could not overcome the vote favoring annexation, with Cleveland replaced as President on March 4, 1897, by William McKinley, who came to office with an expansionist agenda. On July 7, 1898, an act of Congress declared Hawaiʻi to be a territory of the United States.

The news of annexation was a day of mourning for the Queen and her supporters gathered at Washington Place. It came with the nation still mourning the passing of Princess Kaʻiulani, Liliʻuokalani's last blood relative, at twenty-three. Heir to a lost throne, she valiantly supported her aunt's pursuit of restoration, adding the poignant vision of a beautiful, innocent princess to the narrative.

For Liliʻuokalani, annexation meant redirecting legal efforts to American courts, aiming at restoring lands or providing compensation for the millions of acres of Crown Lands that Liliʻuokalani claimed as hers as Hawaiʻi's last monarch. First taken by the PG, then the Republic, in 1898 they were transferred to the American Territorial government. As the new century dawned, Liliʻuokalani took her case to court in proceedings that involved the last decade of her life.

Liliʻuokalani, July 6, 1898. Isolated by her royal status, the loss of family and friends, and the momentum of events beyond her control, she faced the last decade of her life as a regal presence ready to seek justice and in the process provide inspiration.

"*I, Liliuokalani of Hawaii…by the grace of God Queen of the Hawaiian Islands…do hereby protest the ratification of a certain treaty which, so I have been informed, has been signed at Washington, by Messrs Hatch, Thurston and Kinney, purporting to cede these islands to the territory and dominion of the United States. I declare such treaty to be an act of wrong toward the native and part-native People of Hawaii, an invasion of rights of the ruling chiefs, in violation of international rights toward my people and toward friendly nations with whom they have made treaties, the perpetuation of the fraud whereby the constitutional government was overthrown, and finally an act of gross injustice to me.*"

Resigned to the past, loyal to a future for her people, c. 1902.

CHAPTER TEN
1909–1917

ʻOnipaʻa... Victory of the Spirit

"I could not turn back the time for political change, but there is still time to save our heritage. You must remember never to cease to act because you fear you may fail."

— LILIʻUOKALANI TO LYDIA AHOLO, 1917

WHILE THE ANNEXATION OF HAWAIʻI CLOSED THE DOOR on the restoration of the monarchy, it opened American courts to Liliʻuokalani's pursuit of legal remedy and restitution. Her suit, filed in 1910 in the U.S. Court of Claims, stated that the Crown Lands now in the possession of the United States had been set aside by the Great Mahele of 1848 for the personal use of the ruling monarch. She also noted the precedent set by the sale of parcels of Crown Lands by her predecessors. The questions it raised involved the very legitimacy of the overthrow, for she was suing for benefits due a ruling monarch. The overthrow did not negate her rights to benefit from Crown Lands, as she stated in petitioning the court:

"That on the 20th day of January 1891 your petitioner, under and by virtue of the constitution and laws of the Kingdom of Hawaii became Queen of the Kingdom of Hawaii succeeding her brother, the late King Kalakaua, and thereupon under and by virtue of the constitution and laws of said Kingdom of Hawaii became vested with a life interest in and to all the rents, profits and emoluments derived from said Crown Lands after deducting the necessary and proper expenses of managing the same."

The government countered that while Crown Lands were used to support the monarch, they had always been passed onto his successors and were not included as personal property in their wills. With the end of the monarchy, with no monarch to support, they were rightfully transferred to successor governments.

September 2, 1909—Lili'uokalani was seventy-one. She had outlived all of her royal relatives and lived in a world changed by technology, politics, and demographics. Nearly twenty years had passed since the overthrow and a new generation had come of age in post-royal Hawai'i. Nonetheless, she was held in high esteem, an iconic presence from the royal past.

Still mentally alert and focused, she was nonetheless aware of her advancing age. Seeking to assure her legacy, she created a trust under the legal supervision of W.O. Smith, once her adversary in revolutionary times now her advisor. The trust was her opportunity to add to the support services Hawai'i's ali'i had left to benefit their people: Pauahi had funded the Kamehameha Schools, Lunalilo's estate supported a home for the elderly, Kapi'olani and Emma had funded hospitals. Lili'uokalani would benefit the community's many needy and orphaned children whose parents were lost to ill health.

When word of Lili'uokalani's plans to make her trust her primary beneficiary reached Prince Jonah Kūhiō Kalaniana'ole, he responded with a lawsuit against Lili'uokalani, claiming his rights as beneficiary to her estate and any benefits she might be granted from Crown Lands in the case Lili'uokalani had filed.

Kūhiō and his brother, David Kawānanakoa were sons of Kapi'olani's sister Victoria Kinoiki Kekaulike. They were hānai to Kalākaua and entitled princes. Kūhiō, groomed for a royal future, had a close relationship with Lili'uokalani who was fond of him. He considered himself the rightful heir to the throne as Kalākaua's hānai son. He had also participated in the counter-insurgency of 1895 and spent a year in prison for his efforts. But the trial turned nasty with Kūhiō claiming she was no longer competent to make decisions regarding her estate or the trust she had created. The courts decided otherwise, although it was some years after Lili'uokalani's death before the suit was resolved in favor of The Queen Lili'uokalani Trust.

Above left: Kapiʻolani's sister, Victoria Kinoiki Kekaulike (1843-1884), served as Governor of Hawaiʻi Island. Her sons, Jonah Kūhiō Kalanianaʻole (1871-1922) (**above right**) and David Kawānanakoa (1868-1908), were hānai of childless Kalākaua and Kapiʻolani. As princes, they were in line for the throne after Liliʻuokalani and Kaʻiulani. Both played prominent roles in the transition to American rule. A Honolulu newspaper reports the marriage of Kawānanakoa to Campbell heiress Abigail Campbell (**right**). In 1910, in a nasty court case, Kūhiō unsuccessfully sought to have himself (as heir to the throne), declared heir to Liliʻuokalani's estate, which she had willed to the Queen Liliʻuokalani Trust. Liliʻuokalani's will prevailed after lengthy court challenges.

MISS ABIGAIL CAMPBELL BECOMES
HAPPY BRIDE OF PRINCE DAVID

Hawaiian Girl Marries Queen Liliuokalani's Nephew---Lavish Floral Decorations and Breakfast Greet Wedding Guests.

Lili'uokalani makes a royal entry at Washington Place, with a card addressed to H.M. Lili'uokalani from her hānai son. To her hānai she remained the Queen, a somewhat remote figure. They all felt the power of her expectations of them.

Aside from lifetime gifts to her hānai, most of her estate had been transferred to the Trust, evolving into the funding arm of the Queen Lili'uokalani Children's Centers, with pu'uhonua (cultural refuges) providing outreach and aid to the orphaned and indigent Hawaiian children Lili'uokalani sought to help. Tens of thousands, and the Hawaiian community as a whole, have been positively impacted over the years by her foresight.

Hawai'i's Territorial status was a boon to the Islands' sugar-based economy, with more than 200,000 acres planted in cane by 1910. Tens of thousands of new workers were added to the population, most notably from the Philippines and Puerto Rico, both now politically linked to the United States. Demographics told the story. In 1917, the year of Lili'uokalani's passing, the population of the Islands stood at 225,000. Of that number about 45,000 were Hawaiian or part-Hawaiian, which was about 18 percent of the population. But the threat of extinction, predicted since the 1870s, came to an end as intermarriage, improved health care, and a developing immunity to once foreign diseases, provided a reprieve.

Increasingly isolated by time, old age, and the changes overtaking Hawai'i, Lili'uokalani turned to Curtis 'Iaukea. Born in 1855, he was raised

Above: A political cartoon. Teacher Uncle Sam and his unruly colonial brood. There were mixed feelings about how to handle America's colonial expansion. **Below left:** Curtis ʻIaukea (1855-1940), trained from childhood to serve the royal family, involved himself in Liliʻuokalani's life after her Trust had been established, stabilizing her finances and seeing to her care. After the overthrow he was an influential official in the regimes that followed. **right:** Sanford Dole is on the left, Territorial Governor Pinkham on the right, with Royal Hawaiian Bandmaster Henry Berger behind, c. 1914, celebrating her friend Henry Berger's birthday.

to serve the ruling ali'i. Part of Kalākaua's administration, he served as Queen Kapi'olani's translator. Well-liked and respected, Lili'uokalani trusted him for his integrity and for the link he provided to a long-ago past. 'Iaukea assured that her finances were in order and her needs were met. She also became closer with Lydia Aholo, her hānai daughter, who spent time with Lili'uokalani and became her well-appreciated confidant in the last years of her life.

It was not until 1911 that the Territorial government granted Lili'uokalani an annual stipend of $12,000 that supplemented income from her private

" *Lydia, whom (Liliuokalani saw) only infrequently, was prim, respectful, but above all strangely 'independent.' Lydia, perhaps more than the boys, had felt 'less royal...Lydia had taken a step backward from the 'princes' because for many years she believed that both Aimoku and Kaipo were… (sons of)… John Dominis … This relationship placed them closer to the queen's love in (Lydia's) mind … "*

—CURTIS 'IAUKEA

Lydia Aholo (1875-1976), her first hānai, would become her confidant in her last years, creating a sense of closeness that had not always been the case.

Lili'uokalani with her hānai sons, Joseph Kaipo 'Ae'a and John 'Aimoku Dominis.

"*Kaipo was an accomplished pianist, by nature, not study, and (he) enchanted Queen Liliuokalani with music, song, laughter and gaiety. He was the perfect hanai son for her — carefree, always joking, spending money without regard. From birth he had been Liliuokalani's favorite, and still was.*"

—CURTIS 'IAUKEA

Above: Joseph 'Ae'a was Lili'uokalani's favorite. He died in 1913. **Below:** John 'Aimoku Dominis died six months before Lili'uokalani in 1917.

"*Early in November of 1909, I received a telephone message from John Aimoku, one of the queen's wards, saying that the queen wished to see me ... I found the queen with Aimoku sitting in the back parlor. Greetings over, she started the conversation by saying that she was planning to sail for the mainland in a few days to make one more effort to obtain recompense from the Congress for the loss of the Crown Land revenues since her dethronement, and wished (me) to take charge of her personal and business affairs...*"

—CURTIS 'IAUKEA

"The Queen ... asked Mr. Smith for some suggestion, and he then said, he thought it would be a beautiful idea to make provision, in a spirit of charity, for the benefit of Hawaiian orphan children, telling her there was no institution of that sort in Honolulu, and that the need of such an institution was apparent every day to those who kept in touch with the Hawaiian people, who knew their poverty and environment. The Queen thought the suggestion a wise one (and) said so..."

—CURTIS 'IAUKEA

In a wicker chair, as in her first photo sixty-five years earlier, Lili'uokalani at seventy-five.

land holdings, which Curtis 'Iaukea monitored. A generous benefactor to others over the years, professional management of her estate restored her to financial security. At her death her estate was valued at about $200,000 (about $5-million in contemporary dollars) that included ten acres in the heart of Waikīkī and about 1,000 acres in Kailua-Kona on the Big Island—assets today valued in the hundreds of millions of dollars.

As she reached her mid-70s Lili'uokalani, still the Queen in the hearts of her people, became noticeably frail and less connected to the world around her—not surprising considering the times she'd been born into and the changes that had transformed Hawai'i. Without accepting justification for the coup, she had reconciled herself to Hawai'i's changed circumstances, never surrendering the right of her people to pursue justice and retain their cultural identity.

Lili'uokalani with her beloved dog, Poni, on the shaded lānai at Washington Place shortly before her death. Weakened physically and mentally, she died in her second story bedroom on the morning of November 11, 1917.

She celebrated her 78th birthday on September 2, 1917, slowly weakening in the months that followed. On November 11, bed-ridden and frail, Lili'uokalani, Hawai'i's last queen and an inspiration to her people, died at Washington Place. A journey begun in the 1830s had drawn to a close.

Thousands watched her funeral procession as it made its way from Kawaiaha'o Church to 'Iolani Palace where a funeral service was held, to Mauna 'Ala where she was placed in an underground crypt with Kalākaua, Likelike, Ka'iulani, and others of the royal family including John Dominis. Pauahi is with her Kamehameha kin elsewhere at Mauna 'Ala.

Lili'uokalani's death made news around the world, her passing a reminder of times when a Polynesian queen ruled a mid-Pacific kingdom, as this report in the Idaho Statesman reveals:

HONOLULU (IP)—Queen Liliuokalani of Hawaii, whose death had been expected for several days, passed away Sunday morning. The queen had been in bad health for many months. A week ago she began to fail rapidly and last Thursday physicians announced that the end was near… The body will lie in state in the Kawaiahao church until next Saturday, when it will be removed to the throne room of the palace, where the funeral services will be held. As the last funeral of a native monarch in Hawaii all the pomp of the old days will be revived and ancient customs observed…With the death of Queen Liliuokalani has passed the last vestige of royalty in the Hawaiian islands. …But notwithstanding her effacement from public affairs, Queen Liliuokalani never abandoned her regal pose nor lost the affection of her former subjects, and continued to her death a most Interesting personality.

"Onipa'a…Be steadfast," she proclaimed, leading by example. So it is that today, more than a century after her short two-year reign, she is still the Queen, a symbol of grace under fire, the steadfast pursuit of her birthright and the cause of her people. It is unlikely she could have done more once the flow of history had overtaken the Kingdom of Hawai'i and its steadfast Queen.

Above: Lying in State at Kawaiahaʻo Church, followed by a full State funeral at the command of Territorial Governor Lucius Pinkham. Below: Thousands lined the streets as the elaborate procession made its way to Mauna ʻAla where Liliʻuokalani was laid to rest in the Kalākaua family crypt.

In the end, even those who once reviled her were now admirers, aware of the grace under fire and her courageous pursuit of knowledge and of justice. Dealt a difficult hand by the times in which she lived and ruled, she had proven open-minded, intelligent, and dignified. Rooted in Hawai'i's soil, missionary training made her a hybrid—culturally conversant in two worlds, an inspiration to her people, and an iconic symbol of the Hawaiian past.

Birthday offerings beside Lili'uokalani's tomb in the Kalākaua family crypt at Mauna 'Ala. Dominis is to the left, Leleiōhoku to the right, and her parents above. Kalākaua and Kapi'olani are adjacent.

Above, top left: Lei honor Lili'uokalani's birthday at 'Iolani Palace. **top right:** A poster links the Queen and some of the tens of thousands of beneficiaries of the Queen Lili'uokalani Trust. Created in 1909, the Trust supports the Queen Lili'uokalani Children's Centers, benefitting orphaned and destitute children, with preference given to those of Hawaiian ancestry, generously fulfilling the Queen's role as benefactor to her people. **Above:** Queen Lili'uokalani Park in Hilo.

Above: A plaque dedicated to Lili'uokalani at Washington Place, her home for much of her life.
Below: Young dancers at the Queen Lili'uokalani Keiki Hula Festival.

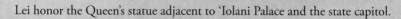
Lei honor the Queen's statue adjacent to ʻIolani Palace and the state capitol.

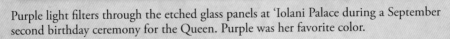

Purple light filters through the etched glass panels at 'Iolani Palace during a September second birthday ceremony for the Queen. Purple was her favorite color.

Notable Figures
IN LILI'UOKALANI'S LIFE
(in the order in which they appear in the book)

'Aikanaka (d. 1837)
Lili'uokalani's grandfather, a high chief. She is born in his house at the base of Punchbowl.

Kapa'akea (1815–1866)
Biological father of Lili'uokalani. He and his wife had over ten children, some of whom died young. All his children were hānai to royal families, including Lili'uokalani, David Kalākaua, Leleiōhoku, and Miriam Likelike.

Keohokālole (1816–1869)
Daughter of High Chief 'Aikanaka and biological mother of Lili'uokalani. Although of higher rank than her cousin, Kapa'akea, they were married to keep the bloodline intact.

Konia (1808–1857)
Granddaughter of Kamehameha I and hānai mother of Lili'uokalani.

Abner Pākī (1808–1855)
Hānai father of Lili'uokalani. Along with his wife, Konia, they greatly influenced Lili'uokalani in embracing her Hawaiian culture serving as a foundation of her Hawaiian identity and cultural perpetuation.

Elizabeth Kīna'u (1805–1839)
Daughter to Kamehameha I, she gives birth to Victoria Kamāmalu the same year Lili'uokalani is born. Kīna'u was given the honor of naming Lili'uokalani.

Victoria Kamāmalu (1838–1866)
Only two months younger than her hānai cousin, Lili'uokalani, they attended the Chief's Children's School together.

Amos Starr Cooke (1810–1871) & Juliette Montague Cooke (1812–1896)

First teachers of the Chiefs' Children's School established in 1839. Their students were all of royal lineage including Liholiho, Kauikeaouli, Victoria Kamāmalu, Bernice Pauahi, and Lili'uokalani.

Kamehameha III, Kauikeaouli (1814–1854)

Second son of Queen Keopuolani and Kamehameha I, Kauikeaouli was in the thirteenth year of his twenty-nine year reign when Lili'uokalani was born. He and Queen Kalama lost two children in infancy, taking as hānai his nephews, Lot and Alexander Liholiho, as well as Victoria Kamāmalu and Lili'uokalani's baby sister, Ka'imina'auao.

Bernice Pauahi Bishop (1831–1884)

Granddaughter of Kamehameha I and daughter to Konia and Abner Pākī, she was Lili'uokalani's hānai sister and attended the Chiefs' Children's School with her. A role model to Lili'uokalani, Bernice defied her parents' wish to marry Lot Kamehameha and instead married Charles Reed Bishop in 1850. This perhaps gave Lili'uokalani the courage to also break with tradition and marry John Own Dominis in 1862.

Kamehameha IV, Alexander Liholiho (1834–1863)

Son of Elizabeth Kīna'u and Mataio Kekūanaō'a, brother to Victoria Kamāmalu he also attended the Chief's Children's School with Lili'uokalani. He reigned as Kamehameha IV from 1855 to 1863. He and his wife, Emma Rooke, had a son, Albert Edward Kauikeaouli Leiopapa, who died at the age of four in 1862.

Queen Emma (1836–1885)

Married to Alexander Liholiho (Kamehameha IV) and mother to Prince Albert. As queen, she established the Queen's Hospital, founded St. Andrew's Cathedral, St. Andrew's Priory School for Girls, and later 'Iolani School. After the death of her son and husband, she and Kalākaua vied for the throne. Kalākaua won the royal election and Queen Emma remained a widow focusing on her humanitarian work. Her relationship with Lili'uokalani was adversely affected by the contentious election.

Prince Albert Edward Kauikeaouli Leiopapa (1858–1862)

Son to Kamehameha IV and Queen Emma who died at the young age of four.

Kamehameha V, Lot Kapuāiwa Kamehameha (1830–1872)

Brother to Alexander Liholiho and Victoria Kamāmalu, he also attended the Chiefs' Children's School. After he was rejected by Bernice Pauahi he was a potential partner for Liliʻuokalani, but she chose to marry foreign-born John Owen Dominis. Soon after, Lot Kamehameha's reign began in 1863 and ended when he died in 1874.

William Lunalilo (1835–1874)

He sought to marry Liliʻuokalani despite being betrothed to Victoria Kamāmalu, his cousin. He was elected king in 1873, dying without an heir after reigning for only thirteen months.

John Owen Dominis (1832–1891)

On September 16, 1862, he married Liliʻuokalani. Despite a difficult marriage, he remained a loyal, well-informed political advisor to Kamehameha V and Kalākaua, serving as governor of both Oʻahu and Maui.

Mary Dominis (1803–1889)

John Owen Dominis' mother and Liliʻuokalani's mother-in-law who competed with Liliʻuokalani for John's affections. She lived with them until her death in 1889.

David Kalākaua (1836–1891)

Brother of Liliʻuokalani. Kalākaua was elected king in 1874 after the death of William Lunalilo. He was trained as a lawyer and admitted to the bar in 1870. He had served in various capacities under two kings and felt prepared to assume the role as monarch. He worked to firmly reestablish and reconfirm the monarchy. He named William Pitt Leleiōhoku as his heir, but when Leleiōhoku passed away prematurely, he named Liliʻuokalani. Kalākaua died in San Francisco on January 20, 1891. Liliʻuokalani took the oath as Queen designate on January 29, 1891.

Queen Kapiʻolani (1834–1899)

Married David Kalākaua in 1863. Having no biological children, she adopted her sister Victoria Kinoiki Kekaulike's two sons, David Kawānanakoa and Jonah Kūhiō Kalanianaʻole. Her other sister, Poʻomaikēlani, adopted Victoria's third son, Edward Abnel Keliʻiahonui. Kapiʻolani traveled to London with Liliʻuokalani to Queen Victoria's 50th Jubilee celebration in 1887. She established the Kapiʻolani Maternity Home and Kapiʻolani Park in Waikīkī was named for her.

Miriam Likelike (1851–1887)

Lili‘uokalani's sister. She was hānai by a couple on the Island of Hawai‘i but returned to O‘ahu at the age of six. She married Archibald Scott Cleghorn in 1870 and gave birth to their daughter, Princess Ka‘iulani, in 1875.

Victoria Ka‘iulani (1875–1899)

Born to Miriam Likelike and Archibald Cleghorn in 1875. Ka‘iulani was named heir apparent to the throne by Lili‘uokalani. She was regarded as delicate with refined manners, typical of the Victorian era in which she lived. She attended boarding school in England, further grooming her for the throne. After Lili‘uokalani was released from prison, Ka‘iulani met Cleghorn and Lili‘uokalani in Washington D.C. to petition for the return of the monarchy. Unsuccessful, she returned to the islands. Unfortunately, she passed away in 1899 after riding in Waimea in the rain, developing a fever that left her weak and bedridden.

Ruth Ke‘elikōlani (1826–1883)

Half-sister to Alexander Liholiho (Kamehameha IV), Lot Kamehameha (Kamehameha V), and Princess Victoria Kamāmalu and godmother to Princess Ka‘iulani. She took Lili‘uokalani's youngest brother, Leleiōhoku II, as her hānai son.

Prince William Pitt Leleiōhoku II (1854–1877)

Lili‘uokalani's youngest brother. Adopted by Ruth Ke‘elikōlani, he was named after her late husband. After his death, with no heirs, Ke‘elikōlani willed the land passed down to her by the Kamehamehas to Bernice Pauahi who then established the Bernice Pauahi Bishop Estate. The death of Leleiōhoku in 1877 positioned Lili‘uokalani to the throne.

Lydia Aholo (1878–1979)

Lili‘uokalani's namesake and hānai daughter. Her birth father, Luther Aholo, was secretary to the Governor of Maui, John Owen Dominis, who was Lili‘uokalani's husband.

John ‘Aimoku Dominis (1883–1917)

The unacknowledged son of John Owen Dominis and Mary Purdy, a retainer in Lili‘uokalani's court. In 1910 Lili‘uokalani adopted him and changed his name to John ‘Aimoku Dominis, officially acknowledging his parentage.

Joseph Kaipo ʻAeʻa (1882–1914)
Liliʻuokalani's hānai son. His birth parents, Joseph Kapaeau ʻAeʻa and Kaheo ʻAeʻa, were retainers of Liliʻuokalani. She referred to him as Kaipo.

Curtis ʻIaukea (1855–1940)
After the overthrow, ʻIaukea became the trusted secretary and guardian to the deposed Queen. He had been in the royal court during much of his career. Through his efforts, he was able restore Liliʻuokalani's finances and remained her steadfast assistant until her death. ʻIaukea proposed establishing the Liliʻuokalani Trust to help orphaned children.

Chronology
SIGNIFICANT EVENTS IN LILIʻUOKALANI'S LIFE

1838	Liliʻuokalani is born Liliu Loloku Walania Wewehi Kamakaeha on September 2. She is hānai to Pākī and Konia and is renamed Lydia Pākī.
1840	Kamehameha III promulgates an enlightened constitution that defines the rights of chiefs and commoners, grants religious freedom, establishes the rule of law, and creates a legislative and judicial balance to royal power.
1843	Liliʻuokalani attends the Chiefs Children's School, or Royal School.
	A smallpox epidemic takes thousands of Native Hawaiian lives.
1848	Hawaiʻi's communally held lands, distributed by a hierarchy of aliʻi administrators, is replaced by private, deeded ownership in a process called the Great Mahele (Division).
	Kaʻiminaʻauao, Liliʻuokalani's sister, dies in a measles epidemic. The epidemic leads to the closing of the Chief's Children's School.

1850	Bernice Pauahi, Lili'uokalani's hānai sister, marries Charles Reed Bishop.
1852	James Kaliokalani, Lili'uokalani's brother, dies at the age of sixteen.
1854	Kauikeaouli (Kamehameha III) dies and leaves the kingdom in the hands of his twenty-year-old hānai son, Alexander Liholiho.
1855	Alexander Liholiho (Kamehameha IV) becomes king. Abner Pākī, Lili'uokalani's hānai father, dies.
1856	Alexander Liholiho (Kamehameha IV) marries Emma Rooke with Lili'uokalani in the wedding party.
1857	Konia, Lili'uokalani's hānai mother, dies. Lili'uokalani remains with the Bishops at Haleakalā, inherited by Pauahi when her father died.
1858	Prince Albert Edward Kaukeaouli Leiopapa is born on May 20 to Kamehameha IV and Queen Emma.
1862	Prince Albert dies suddenly on August 27. Lydia Pākī marries John Owen Dominis on September 16.
1863	Alexander Liholiho (Kamehameha IV) dies and Lot Kamehameha assumes the title of Kamehameha V.
1867	The first printing of *He Mele Lāhui Hawai'i (Song of the Hawaiian Nation)*, composed by Lili'uokalani at Kalākaua's request, provides the kingdom with an anthem.
1872	Lot Kamehameha (Kamehameha V) dies on December 11 without an heir.
1874	William Lunalilo dies without an heir. Kalākaua elected king. Lili'uokalani named a princess. Miriam Likelike and Archibald Cleghorn welcome the birth of their daughter, Victoria Ka'iulani.

1877	Leleiōhoku dies of rheumatic fever and Liliʻuokalani is designated heir apparent by Kalākaua.
1878	Liliʻuokalani composes *Aloha ʻOe (Farewell to Thee)*.
	Liliʻuokalani adopts Lydia Aholo, daughter of Luther Aholo who served as secretary to John Dominis.
1881	Liliʻuokalani serves as regent while Kalākaua is on a world tour.
1882	Liliʻuokalani adopts Joseph Kaipo ʻAeʻa, son of a retainer in her court.
1883	King Kalākaua and Queen Kapiʻolani have a coronation ceremony at the newly built ʻIolani Palace.
	Liliʻuokalani hānais John Dominis ʻAimoku, son of John Owen Dominis and Mary Purdy, a retainer in Liliʻuokalani's court.
1887	Princess Liliʻuokalani and Queen Kapiʻolani attend Queen Victoria's Golden Jubilee in London.
	A new reciprocity treaty is signed between Hawaiʻi and the United States granting the U.S. exclusive naval rights to Pearl Harbor.
1889	Mary Dominis, Liliʻuokalani's mother-in-law, dies.
1891	King Kalākaua dies on January 20 in San Francisco.
	Liliʻuokalani is sworn in as Queen on January 29 and names her niece, Princess Kaʻiulani, as heir apparent.
	Liliʻuokalani's husband, John Owen Dominis, dies on August 27.
1892	The Committee of Safety forms with the purpose of dethroning the Queen and forming a Provisional Government as a prelude to annexation of Hawaiʻi to the United States. By January 17, the Committee takes over the government building without resistance and proclaims the Provisional Government.
1893	The Queen surrenders her throne to the United States on January 24, hoping that her rule will be restored by Washington D.C.

1894	The Republic of Hawai'i is proclaimed on July 4 with Sanford Dole sworn in as President.
1895	The Rebellion of 1895 is led by Robert Wilcox on January 6.
	Queen Lili'uokalani is arrested on January 16 and charged with misprision of treason.
	Lili'uokalani signs an abdication document on January 24 to avoid violence and bloodshed. A military court finds her guilty and she is taken to 'Iolani Palace under house arrest lasting eight months.
	Lili'uokalani composes the *Queen's Prayer* as well as other notable compositions during her imprisonment.
1896	Lili'uokalani is granted a full pardon and sets sail for the United States, returning in 1898. During her time on the continent, she lobbies against annexation and writes her autobiography, *Hawaii's Story by Hawaii's Queen*.
1897	Multiple petitions with 38,000 Native Hawaiian signatories supporting restoration of Lili'uokalani and in opposition to annexation are sent to Washington, D.C., to no avail.
1910	Lili'uokalani files suit in the U.S. Court of Claims, stating that the Crown Lands now in the possession of the United States had been set aside by the Great Mahele of 1848 for the personal use of the ruling monarch. Her claim was denied.
	Lili'uokalani officially adopts John Dominis 'Aimoku, changing his name to John 'Aimoku Dominis.
1913	Lili'uokalani's hānai son, Kaipo, dies.
1917	John 'Aimoku Dominis dies in March.
	The Queen dies on November 11. Her funeral is attended by thousands as they witness the end of a kingdom. Her body lies in state at Kawaiha'o Church and is followed by a State Funeral and service at 'Iolani Palace, with a royal procession ending at Mauna 'Āla.

Index